HUMAN, FLAWED, FORGIVEN

Letting Go of Blame and Resentment Toward Your Parents (For Your Own Sake)

SELMA J. GEIS

Hylosis Publishing LLC
hylosis.pub

Copyright © 2024 by Selma J. Geis

All rights reserved.

eBook ISBN-13: 979-8-89403-004-3

Paperback ISBN-13: 979-8-89403-005-0

Hardcover ISBN-13: 979-8-89403-006-7

No portion of this book may be reproduced in any form without written permission from the publisher or author, except as permitted by U.S. copyright law.

Although this publication is designed to provide accurate information in regard to the subject matter covered, the publisher and the author assume no responsibility for errors, inaccuracies, omissions, or any other inconsistencies. The advice and strategies contained herein may not be suitable for your situation. Consult with a professional when appropriate. Neither the publisher nor the author shall be liable for any direct or indirect losses or damages.

All names and identifying characteristics have been changed to protect the privacy of the individuals involved.

No generative AI was used in the creation of this book's content.

Edited by Wendi Jane Ellis.

To my father.

I'm strong today because I had to be.

You'll never know it, but I forgive you.

Contents

Introduction	1
1. Understanding The Weight of Childhood Experiences	7
Recognizing emotional baggage	
Memory formation and recollection	
Self-identity	
Past experiences and present relationships	
Reflection	
2. The Power of Forgiveness	19
Defining forgiveness	
The psychology of forgiveness	
The difference between forgiveness and reconciliation	
Benefits of forgiveness	
Reflection	
3. Confronting and Accepting Painful Emotions	29
Acknowledging our emotions	
Learning to let go	
Breaking the chains of resentment	
Reflection	
4. Empathy and Understanding	43

      The attitudinal continuum
      Defining empathy
      How to develop empathy
      Putting yourself in their shoes
      Recognizing their imperfections
      Forgiving without forgetting
      Reflection

5. Setting Boundaries   57
      Why is it so hard to set boundaries?
      How to establish healthy boundaries
      Communicating boundaries effectively
      The seven types of boundaries
      Maintaining self-care in relationships
      Severing ties with unhealthy relationships
      Reflection

6. The Role of Compassion in Forgiveness   73
      What is compassion?
      Understanding self-compassion
      Cultivating self-compassion
      Extending compassion to your parents
      Adopting a forgiving mindset
      Reflection

7. The Process of Forgiveness   87
      The five steps to forgiveness: the REACH model
      From blame to empowerment
      Celebrating progress
      Reflection

8. Rebuilding Relationships ... 99
    Opening the lines of communication
    Establishing trust
    Exploring reconciliation scenarios
    Nurturing positive connections
    Reflection

9. Breaking the Cycle ... 113
    Balancing responsibility and forgiveness
    Applying lessons from your journey
    Analyzing the cycle of pain
    Being mindful of your actions
    Reflection

10. Moving Forward ... 125
    Finding your purpose
    Focusing on the present
    Sustaining well-being
    Practicing emotional intelligence
    Structured self-reflection
    Reflection

Conclusion ... 139

References ... 145

Free Companion Workbook

My publisher was kind enough to produce a companion workbook for my book and would like to offer it to my readers for free (without requiring an email signup, as is typical today). You can find it here:

hylosis.pub/pages/free-content

It's a downloadable PDF that distills the concepts laid out in each chapter. You can use it digitally as-is or print it out and physically write in it. Some prompts or exercises include:

- **Confronting feelings of anger, sadness, and fear**
- **Writing a letter to your younger self**
- **Setting each of the seven types of boundaries**
- **Discovering your *ikigai***

Often, we tend to consume information without ever putting it into practice. This workbook helps bridge the gap between knowledge and action, and I urge you to grab it now while it's free.

Introduction

IF YOU CAN'T FORGIVE your parents for something they did or didn't do, I don't blame you. Why should you forgive anyone who has done you wrong, caused you pain, or had such a negative influence on your life? Forgiving them would be like letting them get away with everything, right?

You might even be waiting for some kind of heart-felt apology from them before you decide to try to forgive them—a teary-eyed admission that they failed you terribly as they beg for your mercy. Surely, all your problems would be solved if that happened. You would feel vindicated and victorious, finally seeing the very same people who ruined your life squirm in a pool of regret and remorse.

If only things were that straightforward. The raw truth is that not allowing yourself to forgive has more of a harmful effect on your well-being than you probably realize. While the "perpetrator" may be oblivious or not even care about the damage they caused you, you're left struggling with toxic feelings and thoughts. And as for an apology, what if it never comes? Where does that leave you?

The idea of forgiveness is such a sore point when it comes to parents—the ones who were supposed to protect you from harm and shield you from pain. If they, or at least one of them, didn't live up to that role or were abusive, violent, neglectful, or even absent while you were growing up, they certainly failed you. Not being given the proper care and love that every child deserves could have severely impacted your sense of worth and created damaging thought patterns that have followed you into adult life.

Blaming your bad parent(s) for all of your anger issues, emotional lows and relationship problems might make sense because they are the ones who messed you up in the first place. Perhaps you have even created a narrative in your mind that says it's their fault you can't manage your emotions, have such a low opinion of yourself, or often treat others badly. It's due to them that you can't find a partner, hold down a job, handle money correctly, suffer from low self-esteem and self-doubt, or whatever else it is that creates misery in your life. In any of these situations, these narratives likely hold some truth. But is holding onto this type of narrative benefiting your life?

Now is the time to take back your control. Only you are responsible for your actions, feelings, behavior, and emotional health. While it may seem easier to blame everything on your parents, this thought process gives them the power.

To understand how the mindset of forgiveness (or lack thereof) affects you, try this quick exercise. Say out loud, "I can't forgive my parents," and take a few moments to observe the feelings that arise. You may notice anything from bitterness and regret to rage and hate. These are not very healthy emotions to be carrying around with you, are they? Consider how these feelings affect your outlook on life and how you see your partner, friends, colleagues, or your own children.

Now, think back to a time when you chose to forgive someone for letting you down, disappointing you, or hurting you. Are you able to recall what it felt like to actively move past the hurt and enter a state of forgiveness?

Holding onto painful past experiences isn't doing yourself any favors. Instead, by choosing not to forgive—or by being unable to bring yourself to do so—you keep yourself stuck in a victim mindset that holds you back from enjoying a fulfilling life. By learning and choosing to forgive, you become liberated and free to move forward on your own terms.

Forgiveness is the key to freedom; it releases you from overwhelming emotions like anger, despair, and bitterness—replacing them with more positive ones such as confidence, greater self-esteem, and a sense of pride. It allows you to live life on your terms instead of being defined by how someone else treats you. And it helps you to move forward to a liberated future instead of being trapped in a painful past.

Perhaps you've been trying to forgive your mom, dad, or other parental figure for the way they treated you but haven't been able to bring yourself to fully do so. Maybe it feels like the hurt is just too deep, or your relationship with them is so strained that you no longer have any contact. The channels of communication might be completely blocked, or your current relationship with them may perpetuate the consistent hurt you've felt within that family dynamic. Perhaps one or both of your parents have already passed away, leaving you without the opportunity to confront them and receive closure. The good news is that forgiveness is an internal decision. Regardless of the state of your relationship with your parents, you always have the power to forgive.

I personally understand how difficult forgiveness can be. I couldn't forgive my own abusive, alcoholic father for over thirty years. In my eyes, he didn't deserve forgiveness after all the trauma he put me, my siblings, and my mother through. In fact, I didn't see him as a father at all. *He was a monster, a beast, the devil himself! How could I possibly forgive someone like that?*

Throughout the book, I will share the strategies I used to finally forgive him, as well as anecdotes from the lives of other people who eventually managed to do what they once thought was unthinkable: forgive and move on. Your story is unique to you, but I hope you will find some useful pointers within these examples to guide you as you begin your own healing process.

If you genuinely want to move to a place of forgiveness, this book will help you get there. It will walk through the advantages of forgiveness, discuss how to view others with greater empathy and understanding, and offer strategies to deal with the often-painful path to forgiveness. I can't promise that it is going to be easy, but one thing is certain: once you understand why it is essential to forgive and begin to cultivate it in your life, you will never look back.

We'll begin by exploring the impact of your childhood experiences to gain an understanding of how emotional baggage is weighing you down. Then, we'll dive into the benefits of being able to forgive and the differences between forgiving and reconciliation and between forgiving and forgetting. Facing painful emotions you've long-buried can be challenging, but this book will aim to provide you with a safety net that allows you to let go.

Next, we'll discuss strategies for practicing empathy and compassion. Once you reach a place where you can put yourself in their shoes—while it doesn't negate or excuse how they've treated you—you will find the power to forgive without forgetting. We'll also look at the importance of setting healthy boundaries as you move forward. Should severing relations with your parent(s) be a decision you make, you'll find advice on how to handle this transition without causing yourself greater pain in the process.

By the end of the book, you'll discover how to work through the forgiveness process to reach a place of true empowerment. We'll explore how to nurture healthier relationships, rebuild broken ones, and communicate your feelings more effectively. Lastly, you'll find steps to break the cycle of negative behavior you may find yourself repeating with your own children or others in your life.

As you begin, you may be feeling unsure about your ability to reach forgiveness. *Am I brave enough? Can I really forgive? Do they deserve my forgiveness?* Forgiving the parent(s) who caused you pain may be one of the biggest challenges of your life, but you have the capacity to heal yourself once you realize that the power lies with you. To move past the moments of rage, resentment, and bitterness, the only place you can begin is within yourself.

Chapter 1

Understanding The Weight of Childhood Experiences

"Your past is just a story. And once you realize this, it has no power over you."

—Chuck Palahniuk

IF YOU'VE FOUND YOURSELF unable or unwilling to forgive your parents for the way they treated you in the past, you likely associate blame with their actions. They did something that caused you to feel bad—whether through being abusive, neglectful, mean, unsupportive, controlling, absent, hateful, cruel, indifferent, or any combination of negative actions. You blame them for the way you feel now and may never get over the treatment you suffered at their hands.

Maybe it's your parents' fault you have trust issues, feel insecure, have low self-esteem, avoid commitment, or cannot control your emotions. You may even believe that all of your life's failures are due to them. Perhaps you can't find it in your heart to forgive until they apologize, admit their wrongdoing, and change their ways.

These types of feelings are understandable. It's often claimed that a child's most crucial milestones happen before the age of seven. This idea goes back to the days of Aristotle, who once said, "Give me a child until he is seven and I will show you the man." In this sense, if your early childhood was scarred by trauma, a lack of love and care, or any other damaging parental behavior, it's no wonder you have so many problems today. Of course, parents can also hurt us long after the age of seven and can continue to treat us poorly into adulthood.

Suffering at the hands of a parent from an early age certainly doesn't contribute to a healthy start. Children have a robust set of needs that must be met during their formative years to give them the best chances of growing into well-balanced adults. This chapter will explore the impact that early experiences have on us as we grow older.

Recognizing emotional baggage

We are all products of our past, and our early childhood experience can have a lasting impact on our well-being. Every childhood experience (the good and the bad) has shaped your life. As an adult, many of these experiences will continue to influence the ways in which you think and behave. If you were neglected, for example, you may experience attachment issues as an adult. Although your parents' behavior may have been subtle—scolding you unnecessarily or expecting you to be perfect all the time—everything they did or didn't do ties into your psychological, emotional, and physical development.

The following list highlights some long-term impacts that can result from childhood experiences.

- Emotional well-being:
    - Positive experiences, such as being given love and emotional support, help to create feelings of secure attachment.
    - Negative experiences, such as trauma, abuse, or neglect, can contribute to emotional challenges such as anxiety, depression, or difficulties forming healthy relationships.

- Cognitive development:
    - Stimulation, interaction, and a supportive environment in early years contribute to healthy cognitive development.
    - Lack of stimulation may lead to learning difficulties or failure to achieve academically.
- Social skills and relationships:
    - Positive social interactions during childhood help develop social skills and the ability to form healthy relationships.
    - Negative experiences, such as social isolation or exposure to violence, may seriously impact ability to trust others and form positive connections.
- Behavioral patterns:
    - Childhood experiences can influence coping mechanisms.
    - Being exposed to trauma or adverse conditions can lead to maladaptive behaviors, including aggression, withdrawal, and substance abuse.
- Physical health:
    - Negative childhood experiences may affect long-term physical health, with higher risk of chronic illnesses, cardiovascular issues, and a weakened immune system.
- Self-esteem and identity:
    - Positive experiences enjoyed as a child help to build levels of healthy self-esteem and positive self-concept.
    - Negative experiences, such as being criticized or rejected, may lead to low self-esteem and identity issues.

- Long-term mental health:
  - Undergoing traumatic experiences as a child may lead to conditions like post-traumatic stress disorder (PTSD), depression, or other mental health disorders.

- Educational attainment:
  - Positive early learning experiences can contribute to academic achievements and broader career opportunities.
  - Lacking educational support during early years—due to factors like poverty or lack of parental input—may hinder academic progress throughout life.

Setting blame aside, it's important to pinpoint the early experiences that have stayed with you throughout your life. This is the first step before you can begin to deconstruct unhealthy thought patterns and behaviors. Try answering the following questions, striving to come up with as many examples as possible.

- What emotional support did you get from your parents?
- Did you undergo any traumatic experiences?
- How engaged were your parents in your learning experiences?
- Were you given enough help with your schoolwork?
- What positive social interactions did you experience with family and friends?
- Did you experience violent or abusive interactions?
- How did you react when your parents treated you badly?
- Do you suffer from any kind of chronic illness, or do you get sick easily?

- Did you feel valued and respected as a child?

- Were you often criticized for your behavior?

- Do you often feel triggered by things that happen in your life today?

- Which achievements are you proud of?

As you recall past events, linked emotions may also come to the surface. You may suddenly feel angry, sad, frustrated, bitter, confused, or overwhelmed. Here are three important things to remember:

1. The emotions triggered now are connected to how you felt long ago.

2. Your past experiences are events that happened to you, but they do not have to define who you are.

3. You did not cause, encourage, or deserve your painful experiences.

While you may blame your parents for many of your negative childhood experiences, it's possible that you may also blame yourself in some ways. Maybe you ask yourself if you could have tried harder, done something different, or been a more loveable child. Perhaps you even feel that everything you went through was your fault.

Practicing self-forgiveness is a crucial step in this process. Nothing you did as a young child warranted damaging behavior from the adults who were supposed to protect you. You are not to blame for any harm, abuse, or neglect you endured from the adults who were supposed to love you.

The road to forgiveness begins by forgiving yourself. This involves revising any narratives about being at fault for childhood trauma. A helpful place to begin is with revisiting old memories to better understand how they impacted your emotional development.

Memory formation and recollection

The ways in which we interpret our past experiences influence our lives even more than the experiences themselves. Because of this, uncovering how we initially reacted to negative childhood experiences and how our memories were formed can help us to overcome feelings of trauma.

Believe it or not, our memory usually isn't very reliable—it can be quite subjective. This isn't to say that you didn't really experience abuse or trauma, but that what you remember isn't always useful or accurate. You also may not remember large chunks of your past and may not be able to recall specific events at all.

Memories are formed through a complex interaction of biological, psychological, and environmental factors. They are built in stages—encoding, consolidation, storage, and retrieval—with recollection depending on how prominent they are or how much they are reinforced. Here's an overview of how memories are made.

- **Encoding:** In the first stage of memory formation, data taken in from our external environment is transformed into a neural code that the brain can begin to process. Our senses can encode what we see, hear, smell, taste, and touch from a very early age. Each sensory input is processed in a different part of the brain.

- **Consolidation:** After being encoded, memories need to be consolidated for long-term storage. Through a process of stabilizing and organizing encoded information—which usually occurs while we are asleep—the brain strengthens neural connections, causing memories to become more solidified.

- **Storage:** The brain has various storehouses for various memories. One part of the brain (the hippocampus) forms new memories and transfers them to long-term memory storage.

- **Retrieval:** We can retrieve stored memories in many ways, both consciously and subconsciously. For example, sensing familiar smells, sights, or sounds can trigger memories. Each time we retrieve a memory, we reinforce it, making it more accessible in the future. This means that every time you recall something unpleasant that happened to you, that memory is strengthened.

- **Emotional significance:** Experiences tied to strong emotions tend to be more memorable than others. The amygdala (the part of the brain that is involved in processing emotions) interacts with the hippocampus during memory formation and influences the emotional significance of memories. This explains why, for instance, a traumatic memory that resurfaces can cause you to experience the same feelings of fear years later.

- **Repetition and rehearsal:** The more that memories are repeated and rehearsed, the more robust they are likely to become. For example, we tend to remember daily childhood routines or rituals well because the actions were repetitive and played out often.

- **Personal relevance:** Memories that had a meaningful impact are better retained than insignificant events. You're more likely to remember being beaten by your parents than to remember positive experiences without significant impact. These personally relevant memories are typically able to be recalled most vividly.

Both long-term and short-term memory play parts in our lives, and memory can be either implicit or explicit. Implicit memory doesn't relate to a specific time or place, but rather an automatic response that helps us to drive a car or ride a bike without thinking about it. On the other hand, explicit memory—or conscious memory—is time-space-focused and generally more detailed. We can recall explicit memories and recollect the information they carry, reminding ourselves of places, people, and past events.

Self-identity

Our childhood memories can affect our self-identity, the choices we make, and how we interact with those around us. We often believe that we're who we are because of, or despite, what happened to us. For example, a man who survived a serious car crash may feel that he's invincible or lucky, giving him greater confidence. On the other end of the spectrum, a boy who fell off his bike and broke his arm may grow up to fear taking risks and have low self-esteem. In these cases, identity is built around events that happened and how information was processed and memorized.

As another example, consider my former colleague Pete, who describes himself as a perfectionist. When he was younger, his parents put a lot of pressure on him to do well in school—often punishing him when he didn't get straight A's. Through adolescence and into adulthood, Pete felt like he could only get his parents' approval if he performed at 100% every time. Anything less was consistently met with criticism.

While striving for excellence isn't a problem by itself, Pete was faced with unrealistic expectations which made him feel as though he could never measure up. This led to a fear of failure, preventing him from taking risks or trying new things. Now, as an adult, Pete has a negative self-image and is overly judgmental about his capabilities and achievements. While he is aware of this and often expresses resentment for his parents' impossible standards, he simultaneously finds himself still seeking their approval in his 30s. His sense of self is linked to painful childhood memories of being scolded and criticized.

Past experiences and present relationships

Childhood memories often have more influence over our present relationships than we realize. Negative role models from our pasts can influence the kinds of people we choose to build relationships with and the ways in which we behave toward them. We may avoid people who remind us of a bad parent, or we may be subconsciously drawn to those who exhibit the same type of harmful behavior. This can also trickle down to the ways we treat our own children. Childhood memories of being loved and secure will help us to behave in ways that reinforce those same feelings in our kids, while painful childhood memories can either serve as reminders of how to treat our children better or cause us to repeat harmful patterns.

Attachment styles are based on the theory that the quality of attachments we form with our caregivers from an early age can influence how we later form and maintain relationships. There are several types of attachment styles, and considering which ones you relate to can help to shed light on how you behave in relationships today.

- **Secure attachment** arises when caregivers provide the emotional support you need, nurturing with a sense of security. You're more likely to be trusting and supportive in relationships, and to feel comfortable with intimacy.

- **Anxious-preoccupied attachment** stems from inconsistent caregiving during childhood. Your caregivers may not have been as responsive to your needs as they should have been, leaving you seeking high levels of intimacy, approval, and responsiveness from your partner. You may also worry about being abandoned.

- **Dismissive-avoidant attachment** develops when caregivers are emotionally unavailable or unresponsive, leading the child to minimize emotional connections and develop self-reliance. If you experienced this kind of behavior, you might avoid close relationships and find it hard to trust others.

- **Fearful-avoidant attachment** often arises when a child suffers inconsistent or abusive caregiving, creating feelings of anxiety and avoidance in relationships. These fears may make you feel conflicted—wanting to enjoy intimacy but struggling to get too close to anyone.

- **Earned secure attachment** forms when children experience adversity or insecure attachments early on but later manage to form healthy relationships after mindfully working through past issues. You may have transitioned from an insecure attachment style to a more secure attachment by practicing self-awareness and focusing on personal growth.

These attachment styles are not static and can change over time. It's certainly possible to develop more secure attachments through self-reflection, therapy, or positive relationship experiences. Your path is not set in stone from your childhood experiences. Rather, you can improve the dynamics of your relationships by understanding attachment styles and challenging your preconceptions.

Still, the way we learn to communicate with others is often influenced by our past experiences. If you grew up in an environment where communication was open and healthy, you likely brought these skills into to your adult relationships. On the other hand, if communication in your past was full of conflict, you may repeat this pattern. By stopping to think about how you respond, interact, and express yourself, you can learn a lot about why you behave in the ways you do and start to make intentional changes.

It's common for people to attribute their self-proclaimed trust issues to past disappointments, betrayals, or breaches of trust. While it's natural to feel distrustful after experiencing betrayal, holding onto that pain can sabotage your chances of establishing healthy relationships. Beginning to examine trust issues and putting them into context is the first step to reaching a place where you can leave past experiences behind and start forming meaningful, intimate relationships.

How you handle conflict is another aspect that likely stems from your past experiences. If you grew up in an environment where conflict was resolved through healthy communication and compromise, you'll be better equipped to use these skills in your adult relationships. But if you were raised in an atmosphere full of fighting, miscommunication, and arguing, you may struggle with managing disagreements. Perhaps you avoid conflict altogether—leaving issues unresolved—or maybe you become argumentative and overbearing, causing others to feel unheard. It's useful to think about how you react when faced with conflict; try to consider ways that will help you adopt healthier communication strategies.

These are just some of the ways that your past experiences affect your present relationships. However, very few things are predetermined in life. Once you begin to understand how to separate your past experiences from your identity, you open yourself up to the possibility of enjoying fulfilling and healthy relationships. Practicing self-awareness and self-reflection is key, whether you opt to embark on this journey alone or seek professional guidance to help you navigate the path.

Reflection

- *What negative impact do you believe your parents had on your life?*
- *How much blame do you place on yourself for their behavior?*
- *How aware do you believe your parents were/are of their damaging behavior?*
- *What emotional baggage do you feel is weighing you down?*
- *Do you continue to recall painful memories? If so, are you able to pinpoint why?*
- *Which attachment style(s) do you most closely relate to?*
- *What aspects of your current relationships would you like to improve?*

In the next chapter, we'll dive into the power of forgiveness and explore the ways in which it can uniquely benefit you.

Chapter 2

The Power of Forgiveness

"True forgiveness is when you can say, 'Thank you for that experience'."

—Oprah Winfrey

IF YOU'RE FEELING LIKE there is no way you'll be able to move toward forgiving your parents, you're not alone. However, you may be underestimating the ways in which forgiveness can radically change your life. In an old adage, Alexander Pope stated, "To err is human; to forgive is divine." This doesn't mean you have to be a saint to stop holding grudges. Rather, it explains the profound impact forgiveness can have internally. Think of this as a personal form of internal aikido, where you use patience and calm to disarm your opponent.

In many cases, you are probably grappling with yourself in a kind of shadow boxing while your perceived wrongdoer is unaware of or indifferent to how you feel about them. Even if they repent and seek your forgiveness, you may not be able to give them the satisfaction of accepting their apology.

If you find yourself in this complicated emotional status quo, hopefully this chapter will bring you the clarity you need to change your position.

Forgiveness isn't about the person you're forgiving; it's about you. Therein lies its power. You have a choice: create a fresh perspective and move on, or stay in a boxing ring fueled by anger and rage. Although forgiveness needs sustained effort, it needs decidedly less energy than insisting on staying stuck in a negative cycle. It begins when you decide to hang up the gloves and stop fighting the demons that have taken up residence in your psyche.

Defining forgiveness

From a literal standpoint, the word "forgive" goes back to the Old English word "forgiefan," where "for" means completely and "giefan" means to give. In its early usage, to "forgive" essentially meant to give up, surrender, or completely give away any claim to revenge or punishment. While this might not sound very heroic, the word was most often used in relation to granting a debt or a pardon to a wrongdoer as a way of resolving disputes. In late Old English, it was equated with the sense of "giving up desire or power to punish." Its meaning evolved again over time and was used to convey the idea of pardoning or absolving someone for their ill acts. Today, we equate the word with letting go of resentment and anger—usually inferring the concept of mercy, reconciliation, and granting a pardon to someone.

Forgiveness is a loaded word that can hold a lot of power. It implies letting go of thoughts and feelings of anger, bitterness, resentment, and pain. These often conflict with our desire to seek revenge and retribution toward those who we believe wronged us.

However, the ability to forgive is a primal social instinct. Our early ancestors had to get along for the sake of their survival, so our capacity for forgiveness evolved in the process of natural selection. While the desire for revenge may have been the first thing to come into the heads of our ancestors, resolving grievances and sticking together made more sense in a survival setting.

Today, most of us are fortunate enough to live in societies where our basic needs are met and we don't need to wrestle with saber-toothed tigers every day (although you may feel, in some ways, that you do). The impulse to be in a constant state of high alert doesn't exist anymore for most people. Instead, we have learned to collaborate, cooperate, coexist, and form strong social bonds with those around us. Despite this, we still tend to hold onto grudges and often find the idea of forgiveness hard to embrace.

This struggle likely comes from the complexity of forgiveness. Learning to forgive can depend on making a conscious decision, an emotional shift, or a combination of these.

Let's take a closer look at forgiveness to gain a better understanding of what it is and isn't.

Decision-based forgiveness

Decision-based forgiveness is based on will-power—a willful decision to forgive, let go of resentment, and put aside the need for vengeance. While this doesn't stop emotional pain, it may open up the possibility to separate thoughts from feelings. Instead of holding onto the hurt caused by your parents, you can decide to say, "I don't want to be trapped in this cycle of vengeful thinking anymore; I want to change." When you willfully decide to forgive, you can more mindfully control your future behavior, begin to feel more emotionally settled, give new meaning to a situation, and improve your interactions with others. Although this process isn't easy, you are planting a seed that can thrive if it is tended to, nurtured, and cared for.

Cognitive forgiveness

Cognitive forgiveness is based on changing the way we see things. If we can reframe a perceived transgression into a neutral or positive experience, forgiveness may become accessible. We don't get angry at a storm that wreaked havoc on our hometown, as it doesn't make sense to direct bitterness at an act of nature. While we may experience emotions such as loss, sorrow, frustration, or despair, these emotions are felt as a result of the storm and not aimed at the storm itself. Imagine, similarly, removing anger toward someone who hurt you and focusing instead on how to help yourself overcome the bad experience.

Emotional forgiveness

Sometimes defined as true forgiveness, emotional forgiveness happens when negative emotions associated with "unforgiveness"—anger, resentment, and bitterness—are replaced with positive emotions like empathy, compassion, sympathy, and altruistic love. When we work on emotional forgiveness, we can also change our motives, thoughts, and other associations. We can reduce feelings associated with injustice which often lead us to seek revenge. It's important to remember that we all have the capacity to forgive once we find space for positive emotions.

You may find that you need to combine all three of the above aspects in order to forgive. That is, you need to change thought patterns, emotional state, and behavior.

What forgiveness is not

Forgiveness isn't the same as excusing someone's behavior, condoning it, or forgetting about it. Nor is it the same as reconciliation—this is one possible outcome of forgiveness, which will be explored later in this chapter. Forgiveness doesn't require you to deny or suppress emotions, and it doesn't imply that you excuse the wrongdoer. In short, being able to forgive is a healing process that focuses on protecting your well-being and finding inner peace.

The psychology of forgiveness

The ability to forgive can be influenced by some aspects of personality, referred to as trait forgiveness. It's important to note that many factors contribute to this, and that these can change over time.

Personality traits linked to forgiveness include neuroticism, conscientiousness, extroversion, openness, agreeableness, and stability of beliefs.

Once we begin to work on qualities within ourselves, it becomes easier to modify our attitudes toward others. If, for instance, you have low self-esteem because your parents used to put you down consistently, working on raising your sense of self-worth can vastly alter your view on life. Instead of feeling worthless and unable to achieve, you'll feel more confident about your capabilities, and you'll be more likely to strive to meet your goals.

When it comes to feelings of anger, resentment, and vengeful thoughts, learning how to recognize emotional flare ups can help diffuse strong reactions. Self-awareness involves staying mindful of what you're thinking and feeling, as opposed to letting yourself board a runaway train that is out of control. Being in a consistent state of anger can continue adding fuel to that runaway train—often without you even realizing it.

Perhaps you identify yourself as the kind of person who holds grudges or always seeks vengeance. You may even genuinely wish harm and misfortune on those who wronged you, thinking that you're justified in this thought. Yet, in this scenario, it's likely that you express a passive resistance and bitterness, with destructive emotions bottling up inside.

Active retaliation can cause further negative emotions including hostility, fear, and hatred. It is worth considering why you hold grudges and what results they have caused thus far. Often, anger is a front for fear—fear of being hurt or offended again, fear of not being heard, or fear of not being valued. By assuming a grudge-holding position, you are holding yourself back from taking control and escaping the cycle of fear and pain.

The ability to forgive can also be influenced by our attachment styles, as described in chapter one. As we are raised, cognitive frameworks are constructed. These then dictate our adult interpersonal behavior to a large extent. Studies have shown that people who are insecure, for instance, are often less forgiving than those who are securely attached.[1]

Replaying events in our minds can also play a significant role in how we respond to being hurt, and people with insecure attachment styles are typically more prone to this kind of rumination. When repetitive thinking is associated with intrusive thoughts, it can greatly interfere with your daily life and impact your relationships. If you find yourself constantly rehashing an argument you had with your partner last month or mentally repeating the events surrounding a big break-up, you likely have an insecure attachment style. Understanding this is the first step to breaking through the emotional barriers that may prevent you from being able to forgive.

For some people, ego gets in the way of allowing themselves to forgive. An elevated idea of yourself can act as a large punching bag. The harder the blows, the more momentum they acquire. Shame and guilt may also play a part in leaving you unable to consider forgiveness. Perhaps the pain you feel is so great that it overwhelms your self-worth and suffocates any attempts to regain a healthy level of inner confidence and self-esteem.

The difference between forgiveness and reconciliation

Forgiving someone doesn't mean that reconciliation will follow; these are two entirely separate concepts. Forgiveness is an internal process that isn't dependent on anyone else, while reconciliation involves the restoration of a relationship. Reconciliation is a mutual process in which there is trust, understanding, and goodwill between parties.

In the same way that reconciliation isn't a prerequisite for forgiveness, there are also scenarios where reconciliation takes place without fully forgiving—perhaps for practical reasons such as living in the same home or sharing responsibilities. This means that while a relationship may appear repaired on the surface, an aggrieved person may continue to foster underlying feelings of pain, anger, or resentment.

As an example, consider Ella, a friend of mine who still lives with her parents at age 35. Growing up, her father was overprotective and would purposefully sabotage her opportunities to form romantic relationships.

He wouldn't let her go to school events, was overly critical of the way she dressed, and forbid her from wearing makeup. Ella grew to resent her father, yet she continues living with him because she cannot afford to move out. Although she harbors a great deal of anger and sadness over her father's interference in her life, Ella remains on good terms with him to a large extent.

Phrases such as "moving on," "letting go," and "making amends" are often used to imply that forgiveness and reconciliation are synonymous or must go hand-in-hand. Societal pressures and religious beliefs can also, in some cases, emphasize the idea that both forgiveness and reconciliation are virtuous acts that should be strived for in all situations. However, forced reconciliation is not an effective solution. Instead, focus your energy on the internal process of forgiveness first. You'll then be able to decide whether reconciliation is a viable option you want to pursue. (Though, remember: determining that it isn't is an equally valid choice.)

Benefits of forgiveness

Historically, emotional forgiveness was predominantly talked about in spiritual context. Now, it's recognized as a way to overcome trauma and increase well-being. Psychologists recognize the following distinct benefits related to forgiveness.

- Reduced negative impact and depressive symptoms
- Restored positive thinking
- Increased likelihood to mend relationships
- Reduced anxiety
- Strengthened spirituality[2]
- Raised self-esteem
- Improved sense of hope or optimism

- Increased capacity for conflict management
- Improved ability to cope with stress[3]
- Strengthened altruism and compassion

As the importance of mental health has become more widely recognized and accepted, forgiveness has been acknowledged as a key element in alleviating negative emotions and harmful mindsets. The inability to forgive has been linked with anger and hostility, resulting in serious health effects. Karen Swartz, M.D., Director of the Mood Disorders Adult Consultation Clinic at The Johns Hopkins Hospital, explains, "Chronic anger puts you into a fight-or-flight mode, which results in numerous changes in heart rate, blood pressure, and immune response. Those changes then increase the risk of depression, heart disease, and diabetes, among other conditions."[4] Conversely, forgiveness calms stress levels and leads to improved health.

Studies have additionally shown that people who forgive will experience more life satisfaction and less depression than others. Specifically, "forgiving individuals" are more likely to engage in reflective thinking and have less tendency to ruminate.[5] Rather than brooding over past traumas or pain, they're able to let go of grudges and free themselves to live on their own terms.

Your capacity to forgive is unique; it's possible you may have to work harder than others to reach a place where you're willing and able to forgive. While this path may be challenging—perhaps even feeling unfairly so—the alternative causes even more pain.

While you may not be ready to forgive your parents, now is a good time to start practicing self-reflection. Narratives you create of the past are deeply influenced by your self-perception and the judgments you make. Since memory is a subjective experience, it's easy to convince ourselves that our perspectives are reality and to accept them as absolute. When you consider opposing perspectives about your painful memories, you may be able to find greater clarity and an understanding of what you need to change to move forward in life.

Reflection

- *How do you envision that learning to forgive your parents would change your life?*

- *How is not being able to forgive impacting your mental health?*

- *How is not being able to forgive affecting your physical health?*

- *What needs to change for you to be able to make a conscious decision to forgive?*

- *How much is your emotional state affected by feelings of revenge?*

- *Do you believe that reconciliation with your parents would be feasible? Is this something you want to strive for?*

Now that we've explored the dynamics and power of forgiveness, the next chapter will guide you through the process of confronting painful emotions and arriving at a place of acceptance. As far away as it may seem, you can break the chains of resentment and enjoy a brighter, more optimistic future.

CHAPTER 3

CONFRONTING AND ACCEPTING PAINFUL EMOTIONS

"Our sorrows and wounds are healed only when we touch them with compassion."

—Buddha

FOR MANY PEOPLE, THE idea of forgiving their parents seems unthinkable. Typically, this has less to do with logic and more to do with deep-seated emotions, as parental behavior leaves a strong emotional imprint that's woven into our psychological makeup. Even if you're easily able to forgive a stranger who cuts in front of you in morning rush hour or a friend who forgets your birthday, forgiving your parents may feel out of reach.

There's something sacred about the parent-child bond that, when damaged, is extremely difficult to repair. This can seem impossible to put into words and can bring painful emotions forward that can feel too much to bear.

Acknowledging our emotions

When we don't articulate how we feel, it becomes harder to identify the undercurrents of raw emotions like anger, frustration, and pain. Instead of facing emotions head-on, we let them simmer until they become a fermented melting pot of negativity. We construct narratives in our minds that play out like screenplay—we can't forgive our parents because they did x, y, and z. However, these processes don't allow us the psychological distance we need in order to reach a place of forgiveness.

Anger, sadness, betrayal, disappointment, grief, and fear are all associated with the inability or unwillingness to forgive.[6] In this section, we'll explore some of the negative undercurrents relating to these emotions. You might experience one or several of the following emotions regularly, or you may only notice them when exposed to a specific trigger. However, these emotions aren't always obvious, so challenge yourself to look beneath the surface to better understand which feelings are locked away inside of you.

Anger

While anger is an understandable response to perceived neglect or mistreatment during childhood, it can also present a great hindrance to forgiveness. Anger is a complex and multifaceted emotion that can function as a protective mechanism to create a psychological barrier against further harm. It can also serve as a defense mechanism to protect against emotional pain.

Anger might rise to the surface easily when you're triggered, and it's often the outward expression of deeper emotions such as hurt, disappointment, or betrayal. While angry outbursts may be the easiest reactions, confronting and articulating painful underlying emotions will bring more healing. Like a volcanic eruption, anger allows you to let off steam and release built-up tension, but it doesn't address the simmering lava underneath. Exploding with rage might seem justifiable under certain circumstances, but other painful emotions you suppress lie dormant. This means that while anger is a way of coping, it isn't the most constructive or sustainable method for dealing with deep-rooted issues.

When you become angry, your whole nervous system joins in. The amygdala, a small structure in the brain that processes emotions, releases a surge of adrenaline and cortisol to prepare the body for a "fight or flight" response. The sympathetic nervous system then goes into overdrive and increases heart rate, blood pressure, and respiration as it prepares the body for action.[7]

When anger goes unmanaged for long periods, stress chemicals can eventually cause headaches, digestive problems, insomnia, increased levels of anxiety, depression, and even heart attacks or strokes.[8]

Acknowledging anger through self-reflection will help to set you on the path toward successful anger management. It's also useful to find constructive outlets to express anger. Martial arts, running, journaling, or channeling your creative energy into painting are just a few options to consider.

Try asking yourself the following questions:

- *When was the last time you noticed yourself getting angry?*
- *Can you identify what triggered it?*
- *What other emotions were you experiencing at the same time?*
- *How did you overcome the anger in this scenario?*

Sadness

Sadness is often one of the underlying emotions hidden beneath anger. This can manifest as grief, such as the loss of an idealized parent-child relationship. Sadness may also be experienced as a state of mourning for the absence of emotional support, nurturing, or positive interactions that you desired but didn't receive.

Although expressing sadness may be difficult at first, it can be like turning a pressure valve that releases built-up sorrow, bringing a sense of relief and catharsis. Again, self-reflection can assist you in freeing yourself of the burden of sadness. A few effective ways to start acknowledging sadness are journaling, talking with a trusted friend or therapist, or getting involved in activities that offer a safe space to express your emotions.

Try to answer the following questions:

- *When was the last time you felt intense sadness?*
- *Can you identify what triggered it?*
- *What other emotions were you experiencing at the same time?*
- *How did you overcome the sadness in this scenario?*

Betrayal

When a breach of trust occurs in childhood, feelings of betrayal can be especially persistent and challenging to overcome.[9] As an adult, you may be wary of getting too close to others—in both romantic relationships and platonic connections—for fear of being betrayed again. Not being able to establish trust can eat away at your well-being and lead to issues such as anxiety, stress, depression, and PTSD.

If you feel betrayed by your parents and can acknowledge the impact of that feeling, you can begin to manage the resulting emotions. This might involve addressing the violation head-on or finding ways to rebuild trust over time through self-work and healing.

Take a moment to reflect on these questions:

- *When was the last time you felt intense betrayal?*
- *Can you identify what triggered it?*
- *What other emotions were you experiencing at the same time?*
- *How did you overcome the feelings of betrayal in this scenario?*

Disappointment

When parents don't meet your expectations, disappointment may lead to sadness, frustration, and grief. The sense of disappointment may even be so great that you struggle to form and maintain healthy relationships.[10]

Being repeatedly disappointed can also contribute to negative self-perception, where you internalize the idea that you are unworthy of positive experiences. This can, in turn, make you less likely to take risks or step outside of your comfort zone, impacting your personal growth. Disappointment can also contribute to cycles of pessimism and a negative mindset, preventing you from seeking out new experiences and therefore feeding the vicious cycle of continuous disappointment.

Consider the following questions:

- *When was the last time you felt intense disappointment?*
- *Can you identify what triggered it?*
- *What other emotions were you experiencing at the same time?*
- *How did you overcome the sense of disappointment in this scenario?*

Grief

All children have basic emotional needs for love, validation, and support. Those who suffer neglect, abuse, or abandonment can later experience a profound sense of grief.[11] Some people may grow up grieving silently or subconsciously, yearning for the safe haven they never had.

Coming to terms with feelings of grief is not easy. It requires going through a process of mourning and externalizing hurt that has been previously kept inside.

Try to answer the following questions:

- *When was the last time you felt acute grief?*
- *Can you identify what triggered it?*
- *What other emotions were you experiencing at the same time?*
- *How did you overcome the feelings of grief in this scenario?*

Fear

Fear is another powerful obstacle to forgiveness. Fears of repeating harmful patterns in relationships and of vulnerability in forgiving can be some of the most challenging to navigate.[12]

If you experience seemingly irrational or unexplainable fears, it's likely that they stem from negative experiences in your past. If you suffered from emotional abuse, including verbal or psychological mistreatment, you might fear emotional harm—causing even minor criticism to hurt. Experiencing neglect can lead to a fear of abandonment. Fear of physical harm often leads to a heightened state of anxiety and hyper-vigilance.

Children who experience rejection may feel unworthy of attention or care. They might carry a fear of rejection into adulthood, causing them to fear intimacy and struggle to form close relationships because they don't want to put themselves in an emotionally vulnerable position. Anxiety is also commonly linked to fear, and in many cases, it can be challenging to identify the exact cause.

While fears may be deep-seated and difficult to face, they must be addressed in order to fully heal. Working to identify root causes of your fears is the best way to move toward a sense of emotional safety and open up the possibility of forming healthy relationships.

Finally, consider these questions:

- *When was the last time you felt overwhelming fear?*

- *Can you identify what triggered it?*
- *What other emotions were you experiencing at the same time?*
- *How did you deal with the feelings of fear in this scenario?*

Once you identify underlying emotions and recognize your personal triggers, you can begin to disempower these feelings.

Learning to let go

Self-reflection is crucial to navigating past traumas. By definition, this is a process of purposeful introspection where you examine your thoughts, feelings, actions, and experiences. Taking a step outside of yourself allows you to more objectively and consciously consider your beliefs, goals, values, and trajectory. This ongoing process will help you develop greater self-awareness and a deeper understanding of who you really are.[13]

You may choose to practice self-reflection in a number of ways, including journaling, meditation, introspective questioning, or talking to trusted individuals. Self-reflection will:

- Help you to develop a greater awareness of your thoughts, emotions, and behaviors
- Allow you to critically examine your beliefs, assumptions, and perspectives
- Enable you to set personal goals, consider how they align with your values and aspirations, and adjust them as needed
- Bring a greater understanding of your emotions, shed a light on root causes, and enable you to develop strategies for emotional regulation
- Allow you to learn from past experiences—both positive and negative—contributing toward personal growth

- Aid decision-making by providing a framework for considering options, weighing pros and cons, and aligning choices with your values

- Promote personal accountability—acknowledge your mistakes, learn from them, and take responsibility

- Improve your relationships through fostering empathy, effective communication, and a better understanding of other perspectives

Since inability and unwillingness to forgive are typically connected to powerful entrenched emotions, self-reflection is a way to gently peel back the layers and see what lies within. This is especially useful if you struggle to understand why you feel the ways you do. Once you can reach an insightful point, it will be easier to accept yourself and work toward changing your outlook on life. You may even find that forgiveness will follow as a natural consequence.

Self-reflection can be useful in:

- **Identifying triggers:** Which specific situations, events, or behaviors trigger your anger or fears? Once you recognize your triggers, you can develop effective strategies to avoid or navigate these situations. *Start by asking yourself: what just happened to make me feel this way?*

- **Understanding underlying emotions**: While anger often masks deeper emotions, self-reflection allows you to delve deeper into the feelings that fuel it. Once you understand what is going on internally, you can get to the root cause of debilitating emotions. *Start by asking yourself: what am I feeling, aside from anger?*

- **Examining patterns of behavior:** Pay attention to any destructive behavior or thought patterns that fuel your anger. By identifying these patterns, you can make intentional efforts to change your responses. *Start by asking yourself: why did I behave in that way?*

- **Assessing personal expectations:** Analyze your personal expectations to decide if they're realistic. When they aren't, they can add to feelings of frustration and anger. You can become more grounded in reality by adjusting expectations and learning to diffuse angry feelings. *Start by asking yourself: am I expecting too much of myself or others?*

- **Exploring past experiences:** Past experiences and unresolved issues can contribute to a recurring sense of emotional pain. Self-reflection allows you to explore and address these past issues and separate them from your present emotional state. *Start by asking yourself: is this feeling linked to something I experienced in the past?*

- **Developing effective coping strategies:** Identify and develop healthier coping strategies for managing negative emotions. Options include deep breathing, practicing mindfulness, and seeking support from a professional. *Start by asking yourself: what can I do to help myself cope?*

- **Goal setting for change:** Set specific goals to target the ways in which you would like to change. You may want to develop new habits, adopt positive coping mechanisms, or commit to personal growth for the sake of your overall well-being. *Start by asking yourself: what life-changing goals do I want to set for myself?*

Here's an example of how self-reflection can work:

Years ago, I had to go out of town for a weekend to attend a conference. One month before the event, I asked my neighbors, a sweet elderly couple, if they could help out by dog-sitting. They assured me they would be more than willing to do so and everything was arranged. The day before I was due to leave, my neighbors informed me that they would also be out of town that weekend as something urgent had come up. As a result, I had to cancel my plans and missed the conference. *How could they do this to me?* I was incredibly angry with them for letting me down at the last minute.

For months after that, I harbored a great deal of resentment toward them. I stopped saying good morning to them, and avoided them whenever possible. Eventually, I noticed how this was affecting my daily mood. I was more irritable, often losing patience with my own family over trivial matters. I was being held back in everyday life by my own unprocessed feelings.

I decided to make a conscious effort to challenge my emotions—*why am I feeling so deeply angry and why is this lingering for so long?* In the process of self-reflection, I noticed I kept coming back to the feeling that I wasn't important or valued. I realized this tied back to childhood memories, when it consistently felt like my parents were too busy to pay attention to my needs. Growing up, it felt like my mom was always too busy to give me the attention I craved and my dad was never around. I often spent large parts of my days sitting alone in my room, feeling unwanted and unloved.

After taking the time to understand the origin and triggers of these emotions, they stopped overwhelming me. I realized that my neighbors were well within their right to change their plans, and that they had in fact tried to go out of their way to help me to begin with. Finally, I felt a weight lift—I was able to return to cordial interactions without feelings of stress or rage.

Looking back, I now feel embarrassed and ashamed of how I initially responded to my neighbors—that was a different person from who I am today. However, I share this story as a reminder that everyone goes through life led by subconscious emotions. Unless these emotions are brought to the surface and examined through an objective lens, they can cause us to act irrationally and make choices we're not proud of.

Perhaps you can think of a recent example where you felt disappointed, angry, or saddened but were able to work through it and gain a better sense of perspective. If so, see if you can pinpoint how you managed to do that. Can you implement a similar strategy when you experience familiar feelings of past pain and hurt?

Self-reflection is a starting point toward healing from entrenched negative emotions. While uncovering the roots of your resentment, validation is key. This means allowing yourself to feel and express emotions without judgment. It's okay to say, "I feel angry, sad, bitter, sorrowful because..." By acknowledging your feelings, you're practicing self-care, allowing yourself to heal and move forward.

Breaking the chains of resentment

Resentment describes a negative emotional reaction to being mistreated or wronged. This often happens when feelings of frustration or disappointment build up and become overwhelming. In the process, trust and love are broken—and in some situations, they can never be repaired.[14] When parents fail to provide you with care and support, resentment can follow you into adulthood. You may notice it coming to the surface when you feel you're being taken advantage of, put down, or ignored.

Ruminating about events that caused intense negative emotions leads to recurring thoughts that prevent you from letting go and finding forgiveness. Continually allowing yourself to think about your parents' abusive behaviors can keep you stuck in feelings of regret, remorse, and disappointment. And because certain people, places, or situations can trigger unwanted memories, you may even find yourself avoiding otherwise positive experiences. Although this may seem like a form of self-defense, it's actually an avoidance technique preventing you from getting to the bottom of your issues.

Resentment also shows up in other relationships. You may express it by holding grudges, unfairly blaming others, or acting passive aggressive. This can lead to an inability to build healthy relationships. Holding onto anger and bitterness is often accompanied by a desire for revenge or the urge to carry out perceived justice.

The best way to overcome resentment will depend on your individual scenario, but it will involve finding a way to make peace with past events. Thinking about letting go of resentment may fill you with dread. Perhaps it seems like losing a lifeline to who you are. However, this path will open up a sense of liberation, freeing you from the heavy weight you have been carrying around.

Acknowledging the positives in your life, rather than solely focusing on the negatives, is one tactic to start shifting your mindset in a positive direction. Each night before you go to sleep, try to think of three things you are grateful for. This will help you to wake up with a lighter heart, starting your new day on a better note.

Some examples of things you may express gratitude for include:

- Your health
- Your family
- Your job
- Your home
- Your friends
- Your last meal
- A recent positive experience

Can you think of anything else?

Making peace with the past additionally involves striving to understand different perspectives related to your negative experiences. Remember, understanding your parents' perspectives doesn't mean condoning their actions. Instead, it involves acknowledging that they, too, are individuals with their own flaws, struggles, and limitations. This doesn't excuse any wrongdoing, but rather helps you to put things into context. Accepting, for example, that your father had anger issues, or that your mother suffered from depression, can give you a different take on why they behaved the ways they did. You can then say, "They had their problems. They didn't handle things well." You might even find yourself feeling sorry for them—without forgetting what they did or admonishing them for their behavior.

When you can acknowledge your emotions and even, perhaps, accept your parents for who they are, you'll also find it easier to set boundaries. Setting boundaries is a self-protective measure, allowing you to express your needs, create distance from toxic people, and maintain healthier relationship dynamics. Chapter five will dive further into this topic.

Breaking the chains of resentment involves focusing on your well-being and mental health. Rather than brooding over past wrongs, try engaging in activities you enjoy. Surround yourself with supportive people and make a sincere effort to maintain strong connections with people you care about. Indulge in self-care by tending to your needs.

Freeing yourself from feelings of resentment is a gradual process. It takes time to undo a lifetime of damage, so try not to feel discouraged if you don't see immediate results. As you move toward a place of forgiveness, you'll likely encounter a series of tough realizations.

- You may need to acknowledge that you were denied important attachment experiences by parents or other caregivers.

- You might need to go through a period of mourning upon recognizing that you weren't taken care of by your parents in the ways you needed.

- Your self-limiting beliefs will have to be re-examined; they're keeping you shackled to painful experiences.

- You'll have to shift from a position of feeling victimized to recognizing your parents' inability to provide what you needed.

- You may discover that your parents' behavior stemmed from the way they were treated by their parents, rather than from any selfish desires.

If you can accept that your life has been affected, to some extent, by the disappointments or failures of your parents, you can demystify the negative emotions you feel. You can then view those emotions from a wider perspective and, in time, reduce the sensitivity you experience. By letting go of resentment, bitterness, and anger, you can create space within yourself for joy, happiness, and love.

Reflection

- *Which emotions do you struggle to express?*
- *What emotions do you remember feeling as a child?*
- *How do you handle feelings of anger, and how could you manage them better?*
- *What do you feel is stopping you from letting go of negative emotions?*
- *What would your life look like if you broke free from resentment?*
- *What is one thing you are truly grateful for?*

In the next chapter, we'll explore the notions of empathy and understanding—two key qualities that can nurture forgiveness. This will involve putting yourself in your parents' shoes, accepting their flaws, and forgiving without forgetting.

Chapter 4

Empathy and Understanding

"The opposite of anger is not calmness, it's empathy."
—Mehmet Oz

IF YOU FEEL HATRED or resentment toward your parents, you likely have not yet reached a place where you can fully understand their behaviors.

When a wasp stings you on the hand, you usually don't stop to wonder why, although you will likely remember the painful experience even after the physical effect has subsided. Likewise, if your parents hurt you emotionally or physically, it's unlikely that you will have tried to understand their motives. Instead, you likely continue to relive the emotional hurt, which may have evolved into anger, bitterness, or avoidance.

The attitudinal continuum

Forgiveness is particularly difficult to achieve when you can't grasp the offender's motivations and don't feel any empathy toward them. Psychologists explain that forgiveness takes place on an "attitudinal continuum" that begins with hostility and ends in understanding.[15] This essentially means that emotions must evolve in order for a person to forgive. This involves both an evolution of the ways you think as well as an evolution of your attitude toward a person who caused you harm.

As you read through the following stages of the attitudinal continuum, consider where you find yourself currently in regard to your relationship with your parent(s).

- **Hostility:** The starting point of the continuum is where negative emotions such as intense anger, resentment, and hostility are most prominent. These emotions may be accompanied by desire for revenge or justice.

- **Resentment and contemplation:** As negative emotions temper down, you may begin to reflect on the impact of holding onto them. At this stage, the possibility of forgiveness may seem tangible, but resentment can still linger.

- **Acceptance:** When you recognize that the past cannot be changed, acceptance arises. At this stage, you're willing to acknowledge the reality of what happened, and you no longer feel strong negative emotions toward it.

- **Understanding:** This pivotal point on the continuum brings insight and perspective about the people who caused you harm. Feelings of animosity and hostility are replaced with empathy and compassion.

This is a nuanced process that will differ for everyone. Your path along the attitudinal continuum may not be straightforward or quick. However, once you reach an "understanding" mindset, you'll benefit from a shift toward emotional freedom. You'll be able to decide your path forward—forgiveness, reconciliation, friendliness, or maintaining emotional distance. You'll also feel relieved of the burden of resentment and find a sense of closure, possibly even developing a positive regard for your parents.

Defining empathy

Cultivating empathy can distance you from negative emotions, help you accept your parents for who they are, and lead you to enjoy the liberation that forgiveness brings. Having empathy doesn't mean forgetting what happened, and it doesn't involve reconciliation by default.

In the context of forgiveness, empathy involves "connecting to the common humanity between oneself and the offender, as well as trying to see the situation from the other person's perspective and attempting to understand what might have contributed to the behavior that caused one harm." (Witvliet et al., 2001)[16]

Empathy is linked to the ability to understand and share the feelings of another person. It involves being able to put oneself in someone else's shoes, understand how they feel, and see the world from their perspective. It's a powerful social skill that enables us to connect with others on a deeper level. With empathy, we can foster understanding and compassion, allowing us to navigate social interactions more authentically and effectively.

Have you ever been brought to tears when watching a movie or reading a book? This is one example of an experience of empathy—relating to characters and feeling their pain, struggles, or happiness. Whether or not you've experienced the character's same feelings in your own life, you feel authentically able to recognize and connect with them.

The key components of empathy are cognition, emotions, and compassion.

- When you can understand someone else's perspective, you're using your intellectual or cognitive abilities. In effect, you are saying, "I understand how hard this must be for you."

- Resonating with how someone is feeling involves a capacity to connect on an emotional level. In effect, you are saying, "I can imagine how you feel."

- Compassion involves taking action to help or support others, aiming to alleviate their suffering. Here, you're essentially saying, "I am sorry to see you this way. Let me help you."

It would be impossible to build and maintain relationships without empathy. This prosocial behavior adds to our sense of connection, understanding, and shared humanity. In a society marked by divisions, empathy is described by Stanford University psychologist Jamil Zaki as the "psychological 'superglue' that connects people and undergirds cooperation and kindness."[17] He also suggests that if empathy doesn't come naturally, it's possible to cultivate it. Examples of this include a former neo-Nazi who is now helping to extract people from hate groups, and police officers changing their culture to decrease violence among their ranks.

However, exhibiting too much empathy without regulation can eventually drain you. Taking on too many emotions from other people can lead to burnout. You might even experience a cardiovascular stress response, similar to the way you'd feel if you were in the same painful or threatening situation yourself.[18] This kind of empathy, known as **self-oriented perspective-taking**, is categorized by experiencing someone else's emotions as if they were your own. Because this form of empathy can be problematic, people in caring professions such as doctors, nurses, and psychologists receive specific training to help them avoid being too overburdened by their patients' or clients' problems.

Offering a healthier balance, the best kind of empathy for both the giver and the receiver is known as **other-oriented response**. This is a cognitive style of perspective-taking that allows you to imagine a person's perspective, read their emotions, and understand them. It can lead to empathic concern, such as compassion, which triggers helping behavior. In essence, it requires you to reflect on the other person's feelings without actually experiencing the feelings yourself.

How to develop empathy

Even if you don't consider yourself a particularly empathic person, you can formulate a strategy to nurture this trait within yourself along your road to forgiveness.

You can express empathy when listening to someone else's problems by using these types of phrases:

- "I'm sorry this happened to you."
- "That would upset me too."
- "It's clear that this has affected you deeply."
- "It sounds like you had a very stressful time."
- "That sounds frightening."
- "You are making complete sense."

If you've used any of these statements in the past, you're capable of expressing empathy. You can identify how someone is feeling and relate with them in a supportive way. If this doesn't come naturally to you, believing you're capable of growing empathy is a good place to start.

Perhaps you have no trouble empathizing with most people but haven't been able to apply this to your relationship with your parents. In this situation, it may help to imagine coming across a large boulder blocking your path. It is impossible to move the boulder, so what options do you have left?

- You can stay stuck where you are.
- You can turn back.
- You can climb over it.

Which option do you believe will bring the most benefit?

Staying stuck in one place is not the best way to live your life, and turning back is typically not helpful either. While climbing over a boulder may be scary, this option opens up the most possibilities for a brighter future.

So, how exactly can you "climb over the boulder" and confront your fears through empathy? Here are a few strategies that can be woven into your everyday thinking to help you gradually adopt a growth mindset. By nurturing more empathy in your life, you'll eventually find it easier to understand your parents' behavior even if you don't condone it.

- **Expose yourself to difference:** By exploring different situations, you'll be better able to see things through another person's eyes. You can do this by consuming diverse media. For instance, you can choose to read books or watch movies about people you don't believe you relate to. Or, you may even opt to directly participate in someone else's culture. For example, if you are Christian, you may choose to visit a local mosque to learn more about another religion. Traveling to places you've never been and taking opportunities to experience new perspectives can also help to broaden your mind.[19] In any of these situations, try to be fully present, paying attention to how others behave and respond. This will give you insight into how they are feeling and why, helping you to develop empathy.

- **Read or watch stories:** When you read a book, watch a movie, or watch a show—especially fiction—you can enter the world of diverse characters, getting to know them intimately. Learning about their motivations, interactions, reactions, and goals can be useful in helping you to understand people in the real world. As you engage with a fictional plot and character development, you're using the same cognitive skills you use in social interaction. This is a helpful way to develop greater empathy without getting too absorbed in someone else's life or feeling overburdened by emotions.[20]

- **Increase your levels of oxytocin:** Oxytocin, commonly referred to as "the feel-good hormone", can be increased through intentional social interactions. Playing an important role in facilitating empathy, studies have shown that oxytocin causes change in the brain to motivate prosocial and survival behaviors.[21] Actions that generate feelings of connection, such as eye contact and soft physical touch, are some of the best ways to boost oxytocin production. This sense of social connection triggers you to perceive the other person as a member of your own group, giving rise to greater feelings of empathy.

- **Be curious:** Curiosity is an important component of empathy. This can involve asking open-ended questions that give space for others to express themselves. The more you are able to actively listen and show authentic interest in the other person, the more open the discussion can become. Let others speak without interruption or expression of judgment, and maintain eye contact when possible. Non-verbal cues like nodding can also encourage people to share their thoughts.

- **Recognize your blocks:** If you have an empathy block regarding your parents, you can begin by identifying the times when you struggle to connect to other people. Then, try to relate this experience to any internal obstacles. If you feel triggered by certain words or behaviors, spend some time reflecting on this to diffuse negative emotions. If you've decided that what your parents did was unforgivable, it will be helpful to take a step back and see the bigger picture. Perhaps your reactions are unnecessary, habitual, or based on inner prejudices. You may need to reassess your assumptions or consider if any factors have changed since your initial decision.

Adopting these behaviors into your daily life can help you to cultivate empathy, improve your overall perspective, and build a sense of understanding. Ask yourself how much empathy you think you're capable of exhibiting by reflecting on the following questions.

- How easy is it to relate to others?
- How do I balance my own needs and the needs of others?
- How do I comfort others?
- How do I practice self-care?
- Am I a good listener?

Putting yourself in their shoes

Often, it's not what our parents have done to us directly or intentionally that hurts the most. Rather, it is life events.

As an example, consider Alisha, whose parents divorced when she was 15 years old. The split couldn't have come at a worse time for her. It meant moving to a new town and enrolling at a new school where she knew no one, just as she'd started to find her place in her first high school. Feeling like the "new girl" from a divorced family, Alisha struggled to make connections and felt like she had nobody to turn to—her mother was wrapped up in her own misery and she now only saw her father once a month. Alisha was furious with her parents for ruining her life.

It's often difficult for parents to explain to their children why their marriage has broken down. As a result, many things are left unsaid and underlying emotions are not dealt with. In Alisha's case, it wasn't until she was in her twenties and mature enough to broach the subject with her mother that she began to understand why her parents had split. It took time for her to process what had happened. Her parents had grown apart and weren't happy in the relationship anymore. They had tried couples' therapy but hadn't been able to mend things, and they finally made the mutual decision to end the marriage.

Alisha didn't know at the time how unhappy both her parents had been for years; they always put on a convincing cheerful front. Although 15-year-old Alisha had sworn she would never forgive her parents, she now empathizes with what they went through and has overcome her anger and bitterness.

Once Alisha was able to put herself in her parents' shoes, she understood that their split was best for everyone involved. This ability to place yourself in the position of your perceived wrongdoer takes a big leap on your behalf—a desire to move toward forgiveness for your own peace of mind. It doesn't necessarily detract from the perceived harm done to you, but it does allow you to deepen your understanding of others' perspectives, motivations, and emotions.

We often see ourselves as the hero of our own life story—everything centers around us. *We* suffered because of others. People did things to *us*. Our parents didn't consider *our* feelings. Empathy allows us to step out of that role and visit someone else's life story for a while. We can then benefit from a more balanced perspective and reduce feelings of conflict and anger. The process can involve imagining ourselves in the other person's position. We can also ask ourselves questions such as, "What would I have done in their situation?" However, keep in mind that, despite your best intentions, you might misinterpret or misunderstand others' perspectives. Know that you may not be able to fully understand every decision they've made.

It's important to remember that empathy is about observing and relating to others, not absorbing their issues and negating your own value. Imagine it as examining an old painting. You can see each brushstroke and sense what emotions the artist wanted to evoke, but you can also see its imperfections and flaws. If you don't particularly like the painting, you don't need to bring it home to hang on your wall, but you can still challenge yourself to understand it.

Recognizing their imperfections

The ability to recognize your parents' imperfections can be truly liberating because it frees you from unrealistic ideals about how life "should" be. It also allows you to see that they are human, just like everyone else, and that there's no such thing as a perfect person.

As I mentioned in the introduction of this book, I grew up hating my aggressive, alcoholic father. For many years, I held an image in my mind of him as an evil monster I could never forgive. When his health began to fail, I started to see someone different—a frail old man who felt completely helpless. Yet, despite feeling sorry for him on a basic human level, I was still unable to forgive him. It wasn't until after he passed away that I began to go back and explore his life. Through talking to other relatives, I learned that he had suffered a very tough childhood at the hands of his own strict father. I began to realize that he had grown up feeling undermined and, as a result, never developed much self-esteem. Financial pressures from having children and not being able to hold down a secure job contributed to him turning to alcohol for solace. This fueled his inner demons, causing him to lash out at those closest to him while under the influence.

It was a light-bulb moment when I understood that my father had been a very unhappy man. Once that realization sank in, the weight of anger lifted from my shoulders. I suddenly felt relieved with a deep sense of clarity. And while I cannot excuse his behavior by any means (nor will I forget my childhood traumas), I now understand that he was deeply troubled. He had many flaws and was unable to face his deep-seated issues. This explanation helped me reach a place of forgiveness.

Recognizing that our parents have flaws can be a healing experience that leads to personal growth, greater self-awareness, and the ability to build healthier relationships. It allows us to become more grounded in reality. This facilitates empathy and, eventually, forgiveness. Seeing our parents as the imperfect beings they are can help us to have:

- **Realistic expectations:** When we expect too much, it's more likely that we'll experience disappointment, leading to a higher likelihood of broken relationships. By seeing that people have flaws, we gain a more balanced view that recognizes their limitations and capabilities.

- **Individual identity:** Seeing our parents as distinct individuals with their own strengths and weaknesses helps us to gain a sense of personal identity.

- **Healthy boundaries:** When we recognize our parents' flaws, we're better able to set healthy boundaries with them.

Through empathy, we may be able to appreciate the challenges our parents faced, understand the impact of their upbringing, and draw connections between their past experiences and behavior. When we demystify our parents' actions, it becomes easier to move beyond resentment, opening up the possibility to focus on our own well-being and happiness.

Forgiving without forgetting

> "Forgiving is not forgetting. Forgiving is remembering without pain."
> —Celia Cruz

Although forgiving and forgetting are related concepts, they involve distinct processes and outcomes. Forgiving, by definition, is a deliberate and conscious decision to release feelings of resentment, anger, or desire for revenge. It involves letting go of negative emotions and choosing not to hold grudges. It's an internal process and is associated with healing and emotional liberation. As previously established, forgiveness doesn't depend on the actions or apologies of the wrongdoer.

Forgetting, on the other hand, refers to the idea of putting an offense out of one's mind or memory. Rather than erasing the memory entirely, forgetting for forgiveness means learning and choosing not to dwell on or recall past pain. This is a particularly challenging process because memories can often resurface when we are triggered. Therefore, the best approach is to learn how to remove the hurt from those memories when they do pop up.

Studies show that emotional forgiveness leads to substantially higher levels of forgetting with respect to offense-relevant traits.[22] Yet, you can modify your memories to take away their emotional sting. Usually, it's the memories associated with intense emotions—both the positives and the negatives—that are recalled most easily.

When you pay attention to memories, you get the unique opportunity to learn from past mistakes. Recollecting painful memories consciously can even help to improve emotional intelligence. Remembering a particularly tough period of your life offers you the chance to turn it into a positive memory to occupy your current headspace. For instance, you may choose to focus on the valuable lessons you learned. Reframing negative memories can nurture a healthier self-perception and lead toward a happier life overall.

Here are five strategies that may help you to disarm the power that negative memories hold over your emotional state:

- **Practice self-compassion.** When you're having a hard time, you may be tempted to criticize yourself. Instead, try turning that inner critic into a friendly voice who's like an old friend, there to support and guide you. Taking care of yourself is crucial in the process of letting go of past pain and putting control back in your own hands.

- **Create distance.** This could be physical distance, like leaving a house that reminds you of traumatic memories, or psychological distance between yourself and your pain. You may choose to facilitate a formal "letting go" ceremony where you write down painful memories on pieces of paper and say goodbye as you burn them. Or, you may simply limit your interactions with those who hurt you. Physical distance can also help to cultivate emotional distance, making it easier to move forward.

- **Allow yourself to feel.** Rather than trying to squash painful memories as they arise, you may choose to let them flow. Aim to observe your emotions without judgement, just as you'd watch a cloud drifting by in the sky. This technique can take time and practice to master, but it will provide valuable insight into your underlying feelings.

- **Cultivate mindfulness.** Mindfulness involves bringing your focus to the present moment. When you're present, the past has less control over you, allowing you greater freedom to choose how you respond. A few ways to practice mindfulness are through breathwork, grounding exercises, meditation, or yoga.

- **Go for a walk.** Getting out of the house (or your workplace) to enjoy a walk is a great way to switch off and reboot. Any walk is likely to be advantageous, but getting out into nature can bring even more benefit. Being in a natural environment such as a forest, lakeside, mountain, or seaside helps to reduce stress and anxiety, and gives you a chance to reconnect with your surroundings.[23]

Finally, creating positive new memories is a great way to overpower painful ones. This could involve something as small as treating yourself to a short break or arranging a dinner with friends.

Reflection

- *How much does empathy play a role in your everyday life?*
- *How easy is it for you to put yourself in someone else's shoes?*
- *Do you feel you could benefit from being more empathic?*
- *Can you identify your parents' imperfections or flaws?*
- *How ready are you to accept these flaws?*
- *Which painful memories would you like to let go of?*
- *Which of the previously mentioned strategies do you believe will be useful in helping you to achieve that?*
- *What goals can you set for yourself to create positive new memories?*

As you work toward forgiveness, learning how to set boundaries and establish healthy limitations will be vital. Next, we'll explore how these tools can help you break away from unhealthy relationships.

Chapter 5

Setting Boundaries

"No one will listen to us until we listen to ourselves."
—Marianne Williamson

SOME PEOPLE BELIEVE THAT they can't set boundaries with family members simply because they're family. It's common to feel that we must put up with any and all behavior exhibited by our relatives, and that not doing so would make us selfish and disloyal.

In reality, you don't need to put up with unhealthy behavior from anyone—*especially* family members.

You may generally find it simple to keep your distance from people you don't particularly enjoy being around. Perhaps you limit interaction with unpleasant coworkers, keep your social circle small, or distance yourself from former partners. Yet, applying these same tactics toward family members can be markedly more challenging. When family is involved, it can be much more complex to determine how much disrespect you should endure before cutting ties.

Generally, it's easier to handle non-family relationships because we feel we have a choice. We can pick and choose our friends and partners, but we can't pick and choose our blood-relatives or the adoptive families we're brought into. Parent-child relationships can be some of the most challenging to navigate since the bond is particularly deep. Still, it's possible to stop our parents' influence from having a negative impact on our lives once we learn to establish and enforce healthy boundaries.

When we set boundaries, we're telling others how we want to be treated and protecting ourselves from being mistreated.[24]

Think of boundaries as the creation of healthy distance or separation (both physical and emotional) between yourself and others. This will better allow you to enjoy your personal space and privacy, and your own feelings, thoughts, needs, and ideas. Through boundaries, you shift the focus to your own needs versus the expectations or desires of others. This, in turn, enables a healthier sense of autonomy and self-identity.

In the long term, healthy boundaries will allow you to more easily navigate difficult relationships by helping you:

- Decline things you don't want to do without long-winded explanation
- Express your feelings confidently, with less chance of conflict
- Talk about your experiences honestly, allowing others to understand you more authentically
- Act more quickly, as opposed to keeping feelings bottled up
- Address problems directly, rather than through a third party
- Make your expectations clear, rather than assuming people know what's troubling you[25]

Why is it so hard to set boundaries?

Complex relationship dynamics and emotional ties can often make it feel impossible to live on your terms. You may be afraid of hurting others' feelings or fear that setting boundaries will make a bad situation even worse.

A good friend of mine, Rashid, is an example. His father abandoned him as a child only to unexpectedly turn up years later. This caused Rashid to feel conflicted. While he was still angry about being left to grow up without a dad, he also felt sorry for this man who now seemed down on his luck. When his father started asking him for money, Rashid felt like he couldn't refuse. However, it soon became such a regular occurrence that he began to feel used.

One day, Rashid confessed to me, "It's obvious he isn't interested in getting to know me or his grandkids, yet I feel like I should help him out. He's my dad, after all." While it was evident that he needed to start setting boundaries, Rashid didn't know how. He worried that refusing to give his father money would come across as mean and may lead to losing him all over again.

While you may not be in Rashid's position, perhaps you similarly feel that your parents interfere too much in your life or attempt to exercise emotional control over you. In these situations, do you find yourself going along with their wishes, putting up with negative comments, or sacrificing time to tend to their needs? If so, your inability or reluctance to establish and maintain boundaries is understandable. Fear of damaging a parent-child relationship adds to the difficulty of setting clear limits.[26]

Additionally, societal and cultural expectations about family dynamics can add to the perception that we must put up with our parents' behavior. For instance, the view that we should take care of our parents no matter what leaves no room for setting healthy boundaries. Consequently, guilt can easily arise if we feel we aren't meeting our family's obligations. Being a "good" son or daughter is still a highly valued role amongst many communities, and the idea of not living up to that expectation can stop us from exercising our independence. No one wants to be accused of neglecting or abandoning their parents, no matter how unhealthy the relationship is.

Fear of conflict may also prevent you from setting healthy boundaries. You may want to avoid arguments or tension, opting for a quiet life.

While this might seem like a logical choice, conflict within families can be healthy if it is dealt with in a healthy manner. On the other hand, failing to set boundaries expressly to avoid conflict can be detrimental to your well-being. When established and maintained effectively, boundaries can keep you safe.[27]

If your family dynamic involves dysfunctional patterns of behavior, this is even more reason to challenge these patterns—as daunting as this may seem. You may need to first break free from roles you're accustomed to playing. For example, if you're used to being the peacekeeper, caretaker, or breadwinner, you may find it more challenging to set clear boundaries within your family. However, denying your own needs for the sake of unhealthy relationships, known as self-abandoning, isn't doing anyone any favors.[28] Rather, this can ultimately lead to anxiety, stress, resentment, and even chronic illness. Although setting boundaries can be tough and might lead to changes in the dynamics of your relationships, looking after your well-being must take priority.

How to establish healthy boundaries

Setting healthy boundaries involves establishing limits regarding what you find to be acceptable. This should cover an array of actions and behaviors, including your right to express yourself when things are intrusive, aggressive, or don't feel appropriate. Factors you may want to consider building boundaries around include:

- Respect for your personal/private life
- Respect for your feelings and emotions
- Respect for your principles and beliefs
- Freedom to change your mind
- Freedom from negative or controlling energy
- Freedom from taking on unwarranted blame

- Freedom to say "no"
- The ability to share your feelings
- The ability to ask for help
- The ability to stand up for yourself
- Time to yourself

Note that the process of boundary-setting isn't selfish, and it isn't about needing to get your way all the time. If you grew up in an environment where you felt uncomfortable with expressing your needs, it may take time to overcome that misconception. However, once you begin to enforce boundaries, you'll experience a weight lift as you create distance from unhealthy relationships.

If you're unsure what boundaries you need to set, try thinking about what types of interactions make you feel used, humiliated, invalidated, put down, undermined, frustrated, angry, or upset. Consider interactions with everyone in your life—from parents to friends to coworkers. The litmus test is this: **do you feel happy within your existing relationships?** If not, you likely can benefit from drawing more lines about what you will and will not accept.

Here are some examples of things you may find yourself saying or thinking that point toward needing to set clearer boundaries:

- "My parents expect me to drop everything when they need me."
- "I hate it when my mom criticizes how I dress."
- "Every time I see my dad, he reminds me of how disappointed he is in me."
- "I loathe family gatherings because they always end in argument."

- "My parents never listen to what I have to say; they treat me like I'm still a child."

Three essential tools you need to acquire for setting healthy boundaries are: self-awareness, assertiveness, and communication skills.

Concerning **self-awareness**, it's crucial to be clear about what expectations you have of yourself and others, and what you are and are not comfortable with in specific situations. **Assertiveness** involves expressing how you feel openly and respectfully so people will listen. And, finally, by adopting good **communication skills**, you can convey that assertiveness with greater clarity.

Communicating boundaries effectively

Perhaps you desperately want to set boundaries, but you don't feel you have the tools to communicate them effectively. Whether you've never been able to talk candidly with your parents or you simply don't feel comfortable explaining how you feel, fear may be holding you back. Additionally, you may worry about how your parents will respond. *Will they reject you, humiliate you, or alienate you?*

The good news is that setting boundaries doesn't necessarily have to mean making public announcements to concerned parties about what you aim to do. Still, some boundaries *will* require communication in order to be effective. For each boundary you implement, ask yourself what the result would be if you choose not to communicate it with anyone. If the boundary simply addresses the ways you'll respond in certain scenarios, for example, you may find that communication is unnecessary. However, if the boundary involves enforcing ways you expect others to treat you, it would need to be explained in some capacity.

The following are guidelines to help you in planning to communicate your boundaries:

- Take time to self-reflect before you begin a conversation. What are your values, needs, and limits? Once you are clear about that, you'll be better prepared to express your boundaries with greater confidence.

- Be as clear and as straightforward as possible. Language should be simple, yet specific, as vague statements can lead to misunderstandings. Communication should also be done respectfully, without raising your voice or using verbal attacks. *Avoid: "You're always nagging me; I need a break!" Instead, consider: "I'm going to take this weekend to decompress, and I'll follow up afterwards."*

- Use "I" statements to state your needs or requests. *For instance, avoid: "You're making me feel overwhelmed. You need to give me more space." Instead, try: "I feel overwhelmed when there are so many demands on me. I need to prioritize my own needs first."*

- Assertiveness is essential when communicating boundaries. Still, it's possible to be both assertive and kind at the same time. Express your needs firmly in a way that shows respect for the other person. *For example, say, "I appreciate your advice, but I'll be making my own decisions."*

- When possible, offer alternatives to show you want to find solutions for both parties. *For instance, if you're asked to go to a family event you don't want to attend, you can say: "I can't make this event, but I'd love to get dinner together next week."*

- Highlight the ways in which your boundaries will positively impact the other party. *For example, you may say: "This will help us both to understand each other better, strengthening our relationship."*

- Avoid apologizing unnecessarily for your choices. *For instance, if someone asks you for a favor that would disrupt your day, it's okay to say, "That won't be possible today; I've got other plans."* There's no need to add an apology or give further explanation about why you won't comply with their request.

- Ensure your non-verbal cues support what you're saying, rather than negating it. Helpful actions include maintaining eye contact, standing or sitting confidently, and using a calm and steady tone of voice. Detrimental actions include eye rolling, crossing arms, and raising your voice.

- Actively listen to the other party throughout the conversation. This involves encouraging the other person to share their thoughts and feelings without interruption. Even if you don't agree with their viewpoint, try to understand where they're coming from.

- Accept any discomfort that arises as a result of setting boundaries—whether it's guilt, shame, or remorse. While it may be challenging, the most helpful path is to acknowledge these feelings without self-judgment.

The seven types of boundaries

There are seven distinct types of boundaries you should consider setting within your relationships:

1. **Mental:** These boundaries allow you to think for yourself. They involve having your thoughts, values, and opinions respected, accepted, and validated.

2. **Emotional:** Take a stand to cut out activities or actions that weigh you down. Set limits to be emotionally available to others only when you decide to be and of your own volition.

3. **Physical:** Define how you would like your personal space and your body respected.

4. **Material:** Decide how you'll manage money, including if and when you're comfortable lending it to others. Additionally, consider setting limits around your belongings such as your car, house, or other possessions.

5. **Time:** Determine the amount of time you're comfortable spending with specific people or on specific activities.

6. **Conversational:** Choose which topics you feel comfortable discussing with others and which topics you'll stay away from.

7. **Internal:** Self-regulate the amount of energy you spend on others versus on your own needs. Give yourself permission to take breaks from relationships as needed.

These seven sacred boundaries are all personal; they allow you to protect your own well-being. Successfully maintaining boundaries in all seven areas will help you to feel most balanced.

Pause to consider what types of boundaries will be most helpful for you to implement first.

Once you have a clear idea about what types of boundaries you would like to set, use the following guidelines to help implement them:

- **Put your needs first:** Consider your personal needs. Do you desire more free time or more independence? Build these needs into your boundaries to avoid getting taken advantage of.

- **Prioritize and value your time:** Time is the one finite resource we have, so if a family member expects to monopolize yours, it's crucial to set a boundary. You may do this through stating certain hours that you'll be available, or by setting a maximum number of hours you'll dedicate per week.

- **Be direct, yet kind:** For many people, facing their parents to directly communicate boundaries is a daunting thought. To help mitigate this fear, you can try practicing the conversation beforehand in a mirror or with a trusted friend.

- **Set realistic expectations for relationships:** You can't force anyone in your life to change, so instead you must ensure your own expectations about the relationship are set realistically.

Prepare yourself for the possibility of a negative response when communicating your boundaries, especially if you know that the other party is typically resistant to change. You'll also need to ensure that you're prepared to follow through with consequences in the event that your family members don't respect the boundaries you set.

- **Talk it out:** If both parties are open to discussion, respectful conversation can help to demystify misunderstandings from both sides.

- **Avoid family drama and gossip:** If you tend to find yourself in the middle of family drama, try excusing yourself when these topics come up. This will help to protect your emotional health.

- **Identify and avoid triggers:** What behaviors trigger you when you're with your parents or family members? By identifying these, it will be easier to avoid them in the future. For example, if topics like politics or religion are likely to prompt unfavorable reactions, it's typically best to excuse yourself from the conversation when they come up.

- **Specify consequences:** You might feel like you aren't taken seriously when you express how you want or don't want to be treated. For this reason, it's crucial that you specify the consequences of others not respecting your boundaries. For example, you may choose to limit interactions or even completely cut ties with those who continuously overstep or ignore boundaries.

- **Learn to say "no":** Do you ever find yourself saying "yes" when you want to say "no"? If you're used to being a people-pleaser, learning to say "no" can be a particularly difficult skill to learn. Yet, this is one of the most impactful ways to take back your power and improve your sense of self-worth. You'll likely be met with some resistance when you begin turning down requests, so be prepared to firmly stand by your decisions.

- **Walk away:** When situations get stressful and you feel your boundaries being pushed, don't be afraid to walk away. This sends a clear message about how serious your limits are, and it conserves both your mental and emotional energy.

Maintaining self-care in relationships

Although it's nice to be receptive to the emotions of others, this can often become overwhelming and draining in the context of an unhealthy relationship. This, in turn, can affect your emotional health and eventually lead to burnout. In contrast, self-care involves prioritizing your own needs first. While this may seem like a selfish practice at first glance, allowing your emotional battery to recharge will actually provide you with increased capacity to give back to others.

Here are some strategies you can use incorporate self-care into your life:

- **Begin by establishing boundaries.** As discussed throughout this chapter, communicate limits clearly and be assertive about what you can and cannot commit to emotionally.

- **Say "no" more often.** You can't be available to everyone at all times. Default to saying "no" and reserve "yes" for the things that truly benefit you.

- **Engage in activities you enjoy.** Whether you like running, reading, traveling, cooking, gaming, or anything else, make sure to carve out time regularly for personal fulfillment.

- **Manage your expectations and recognize your limitations.** Acknowledge the fact that you can't do everything and use this as a guiding light to become more intentional about the ways you spend your time and energy.

- **Practice mindfulness and relaxation.** Meditating or deep breathing for ten minutes daily has been proven to help manage stress.[29] This gives you space to detach from your surroundings and become more present within your body.

- **Prioritize a good night's sleep.** Lack of sleep can impact emotional resilience and overall well-being.[30] Conversely, getting quality rest is one of the most impactful ways to care for your physical and emotional health.

- **Nurture relationships that provide support and understanding.** Rather than expending too much energy on the more toxic relationships in your life, surround yourself with people who respect your boundaries and bring something positive to the table.

- **Get regular exercise.** Get creative—join a sports club, take up yoga, or go hiking in nature.

- **Find a creative outlet for your emotions.** Try journaling, drawing, making music, or learning to dance. Each of these allow you to express yourself while channeling your emotions into a positive activity.

- **Be kind to yourself.** Treat yourself with the same compassion and understanding you would extend to a good friend or loved one.

- **Take a break from the digital world.** Continuous connection to a phone or laptop, and especially social media, can lead to feelings of overwhelm. Reducing your amount of screen time each day will give you more headspace to reflect and experience a sense of calmness.[31]

- **Celebrate your accomplishments, no matter how small.** When celebrating, your self-esteem gets a boost and you become more intrinsically motivated to keep working toward your goals.

Tailor your self-care practices to meet your needs and preferences, adjusting your routines as circumstances change. By taking care of yourself, you'll be more available to offer support to others when you choose to do so.

Severing ties with unhealthy relationships

Even when you're aware that a familial relationship is no longer serving you, it can be incredibly difficult to cut ties. It's easy to feel like you can't escape someone you're related to. However, if your boundaries are continuously disregarded or if you consistently feel disrespected, withdrawing from the relationship may be your best move. Failing to do so can mean continuing to find yourself in a toxic or unhealthy situation detrimental to your emotional well-being.[32]

Estrangement from family members happens more often than you may think. Many people choose not to talk about it, fearing that they might be judged for their decision to sever ties. A 2015 U.S. study found that more than 40% of individuals have experienced family estrangement at one point in their lives.[33] A similar study in the UK found that estrangement affects at least one in five British families.[34]

Psychotherapist Nedra Glover Tawwab explains, "Setting limits won't disrupt a healthy relationship."[35] In other words, if a relationship is healthy, it can withstand the boundaries you set. And if a relationship is toxic or unhealthy, it might not be worth maintaining.

When making the determination about whether to cut ties with a family member, you may also want to consider their capacity for change. *Do you feel that they are likely to ever be able to acknowledge the problem and be willing to work toward a solution?* If you've found that issues seem to endlessly perpetuate with no meaningful progress on their part, it may be time to sever ties. Furthermore, if the situation involves physical, verbal, emotional, or psychological abuse, you should distance yourself from the perpetrators for your own safety.

Here are some tips to consider when navigating the severing of ties in a relationship. While not every tip may apply to your scenario, you can use them to help provide a framework.

- **Plan your approach.** How will you communicate your decision to sever ties, if at all? If you choose to directly share your decision with the other party, a calm and private setting typically works best. Practicing what you want to say ahead of time can also be helpful. Depending on the situation, written communication—such as a letter or an email—may be the best option.

- **Be direct and honest.** Try not to attach blame. Instead, you can say, "I am unhappy with how things are going and I need to maintain my distance from you for now."

- **Remain calm and assertive.** Focus on expressing what you wish to say with conviction. If needed, you can set a maximum time limit for the conversion to ensure you don't get wrapped up talking in circles.

- **Limit contact.** Once you've severed ties, follow through by limiting contact as much as possible. This might involve unfollowing or blocking on social media, changing your cell phone number, or creating physical distance.

- **Prioritize your safety.** Abusive or violent parents might pose a threat to your safety. In such cases, seek help from law enforcement or local support groups.

- **Set your sights on the future.** You may have been involved in an unhealthy parent-child relationship for so long that you never imagined it was possible to enjoy a brighter future. Once you successfully sever those ties, focus on all the good things to come and the positive changes in your life. Set yourself new, achievable goals, make plans, and explore opportunities that nurture your personal growth.

- **Allow yourself time to heal.** It's never easy to remove yourself from a relationship, and it can be even more difficult when it's a close one with parents or other family members. Allow yourself the space and time to grieve, process your emotions, and move forward gradually. Rather than suppressing challenging feelings, try to identify and acknowledge what you're experiencing. This may include anything from anger or sadness to guilt or remorse. Emotions can also heighten on days that remind you of the family member, such as birthdays or holidays.

Remember that stepping away from an unhealthy relationship is a significant step toward prioritizing your well-being. It's okay to seek help, lean on your support system, and take time to heal as you restructure your life.

Perhaps, over time, the person you've distanced yourself from will change their attitude or behavior. Consider whether you want to keep the door open to the possibility of eventually making amends. However, in these situations, it's particularly important to ensure you're setting realistic expectations to avoid repeating past hurt.

Reflection

- *Which boundaries do you feel are consistently crossed by your parents?*
- *Do you find it difficult to maintain the boundaries you set?*
- *What aspects of your life could be changed to ensure your boundaries are respected?*
- *What coping strategies can you use to help deal with the negative emotions you experience in unhealthy relationships?*
- *How often do you practice self-care and spend time prioritizing your own needs?*

Next, we'll explore how compassion can help you adopt a forgiving mindset. Even if a relationship has broken down or you've severed all ties, there's still room for compassion on your journey to fully healing internally. Regardless of what happens in the future, finding peace of mind now can help you cope with the remnants of your past.

- Practicing compassion can **break the cycle of hurt and retaliation**, reducing the presence of negative emotions and the desire for negative actions. It can act as a catalyst for positive change and growth in both ourselves and others.

- Through compassion, we can **rebuild or preserve relationships**. Having a greater capacity for connection and understanding makes it more possible for connections to grow and damaged relationships to heal.

- Self-compassion is crucial for personal growth, as it allows us **to learn from our experiences** and move forward with a greater sense of resilience. The negative impact on our mental health is also reduced, bringing greater psychological well-being and lower levels of stress, anxiety, and depression.

Understanding self-compassion

Dr. Kristin Neff, author of "Self-Compassion: The Proven Power of Being Kind to Yourself," defines self-compassion as, "the act of being touched by and open to your own suffering, not avoiding or disconnecting from it, generating the desire to alleviate one's suffering and to heal oneself with kindness."[39] As an example, if you feel inadequate about your abilities or are angry with yourself for failing an important exam, extending understanding and kindness to yourself is an act of self-compassion.

When you practice self-compassion, you can relate to yourself in a way that's more forgiving, accepting, and loving when things aren't going as well as you'd hope. This is similar to self-love but less permanent. Self-compassion is exercised only as needed while self-love is a continuous state of being. Self-compassion is the moment when you overcome feelings of self-loathing for arguing with a loved one, avoid beating yourself up for forgetting to call your friend, or treat yourself with kindness after getting passed on for a promotion you thought was locked in.

There are a lot of misconceptions about what self-compassion means, with many people thinking it is synonymous with selfishness, over-optimism, self-pity, or passivity. In a world where everyone seems to be striving for perfection, the idea of self-compassion can trigger these types of false beliefs. However, in truth, high levels of self-compassion have been proven to equate with more giving behaviors and attitudes.[40] In conclusion, when we're kind to ourselves, we achieve a state of inner balance that makes us better able to meet the needs of others.

We can divide self-compassion into three key elements: self-kindness, common humanity, and mindfulness. Each one plays a role in allowing us to practice self-compassion when we need to.

1. **Self-kindness**: Self-compassion involves being warm, understanding, and gentle toward yourself when faced with challenges or failures. This equates to treating yourself with the same care and support you'd extend to a friend in a similar situation. Imagine, let's say, you accidentally reverse into a parked car while leaving work. Instead of berating yourself, self-kindness involves responding with understanding and support. Accidents happen and although you probably should have been more careful, beating yourself up will not help the situation. Once you have done the responsible thing by reporting the event, move on without scolding yourself.

2. **Common humanity**: Self-compassion also entails recognizing that suffering, mistakes, and imperfections are part of the shared human experience. The Dalai Lama has been quoted as saying, "Love and compassion are necessities, not luxuries. Without them humanity cannot survive." In other words, we need to cultivate love and compassion in our lives if we want to thrive as a species. Instead of feeling isolated or alone in your struggles, self-compassion helps you to understand that everyone goes through difficult times. If, for example, you're finding it stressful to cope with your young children, remember that most parents feel the same way at one time or another. By recognizing

that others experience similar problems, you're less likely to feel like a failure.

3. **Mindfulness**: Another important part of self-compassion involves being aware of your thoughts and feelings without being overwhelmed by them. Through mindfulness, you can approach experiences with an open and non-judgmental awareness. By acknowledging your emotions without getting entangled in negative self-talk, you can avoid judging yourself too harshly. For instance, the next time you get angry at your parents for something they said or did, be present in that moment. Observe your thoughts and feelings without identifying with them too much. Rather, try to see them as small fluffy clouds passing over the blue sky. Watch them gradually drift away as you regain your sense of calmness and clarity.

Cultivating self-compassion

We are often our own worst enemies, capable of showing compassion to others yet accustomed to criticizing ourselves over the smallest things. One way to overcome this bad habit (and it is just that: a habit) is to change your inner dialogue with yourself. Frequently, that inner critic makes us feel worthless, shining a spotlight on our weaknesses and mistakes. When your inner dialogue uses a tone that is harsh and unsupportive, you're likely to experience negative emotions like guilt, shame, and anger.[41]

This vicious cycle of negative self-talk can lead to a downward spiral causing you feel terribly low. But, if you replace that negative inner dialogue with a more compassionate voice, you may be surprised by how much more self-worth and self-acceptance you'll experience. Simply by being kind to yourself, you'll begin to change your perspective on who you are and what you're capable of.

These three steps can help you to change the way you talk to yourself:

Step one:

- Notice when you're being self-critical.

- Note the words, phrases, and tone you use.

- When you read them again, it will make you aware of how little compassion you show yourself.

Step two:

- Begin to challenge negative self-talk by "talking back" to the critical voice in your head.

- Use a warm, loving tone, instead of a nasty voice.

- Tell the voice that while you understand it's trying to protect you, it's causing you unnecessary pain.

- State that you're going to allow your compassionate self to speak for a few moments.

Step three:

- Start reframing negative dialogue from the critical voice by putting it in a more positive perspective.

- Talk to yourself as if you were a compassionate friend who speaks with positivity.

- Once you begin to practice this kind of positive self-talk, you will begin to feel greater self-love.

Many of the reactions that might have served us as children can hinder us in our adult lives. You may find it useful to have a conversation with your inner child to show them the compassion they may never have received from their parents. Somewhere deep inside of us, we all need that tender love and support—and it's never too late to give it.

The next exercise aims to address your inner child by imagining a conversation between yourself now and a younger version of you. This will entail recalling difficult times you experienced and analyzing how they continue to affect you in your present-day life.

Start by attempting to recall difficult times you experienced as a child. Remembering these types of childhood experiences may open the door to a range of emotions including:

- Anger
- Abandonment or rejection
- Insecurity
- Vulnerability
- Guilt or shame
- Anxiety

Once you identify these emotions, you might realize that similar situations in your present-day life trigger the same responses. For example, perhaps you planned an evening out with a friend, but they had to cancel at the last minute due to a family crisis. Although you logically understood, you still felt rejected and angry. You reacted in a childlike way, blasting them over the phone before hanging up in fury.

If you look at this response through the eyes of your inner child, you may see that the disappointment you felt goes back to the way you used to feel when your parents canceled playdates or outings because they were too busy with something else.

You can now address that child, telling them you understand how they feel, how they were right to feel hurt, and how they deserved more. It may feel a little strange to imagine opening up to your childhood self, but it will eventually help you to nurture more self-compassion. If talking to yourself seems too weird, you can also try writing a letter to your younger self.

If you decide to write, begin your letter by addressing your childhood memories from your adult perspective. Offer explanations for painful events that you didn't understand in the moment and try to soothe some of the lingering pain your childhood self continues to feel. Write with tenderness and love, telling your inner child you are there to support and help them.

While it may take a while to alleviate the pain your inner child suffered, this is a good starting point. When you show compassion to yourself, you'll eventually learn to foster greater self-love and inner well-being. This will open the door to forgiveness—for yourself and for others who have caused you harm.

Extending compassion to your parents

As you begin to experience the benefits of practicing self-compassion, it will become easier to show compassion for others, including the parents you feel unable to forgive. Compassion toward your parents is an act of intentional and mindful effort on your part and doesn't necessarily mean you'll absolve them of any damaging behavior.

You may feel like saying, "I feel nothing for my parents," or, "They don't deserve my compassion." Notice that within those words there is still a lot of unresolved pain—pain that is hurting you, first and foremost.

By sitting with your feelings and practicing greater self-awareness, you might realize that your inability to show compassion to your parents is linked to one or more of the following explanations:

- **Attachment and expectations:** The relationship you had with your parents as a child has formed the foundation for your attachment style and expectations in relationships. If your parents were inconsistent, neglectful, or abusive, your ability to trust may have been compromised, making it difficult for you to extend compassion. *Does this resonate with you?*

- **Betrayal and broken trust:** If your parents betrayed your trust or caused you emotional or physical harm, it's understandable that you have deep wounds. *Could your inability to be compassionate hinge on this sense of betrayal?*

- **Shame and guilt:** You might have internalized the negative experiences you suffered as a child and blamed yourself for your parents' actions. While still carrying around these powerful emotions, it could be difficult to feel compassion for the people who caused them in the first place. *Does shame or guilt feature in your reasons for not being able to extend compassion?*

- **Unresolved grief:** If your parents hurt you as a child, this may have led to unresolved grief over the loss of an idealized or hoped-for relationship. As you continue to navigate the mourning process, it may be too difficult to approach your parents with compassion. *Could grief be preventing you from showing them compassion?*

- **Survival mechanisms:** If you suffered abuse or neglect, you developed defense mechanisms such as detachment or emotional numbing to cope with the pain. (This statement, mentioned previously, is an example: "I feel nothing for my parents.") Such mechanisms, while useful initially, can stop you from being able to show compassion as you grow older. *Does this relate to how you feel?*

- **Fear of vulnerability:** To show compassion, you have to be prepared to be vulnerable and unafraid to open up. This can be a frightening thought. What if you get hurt again? If your parents caused you significant pain, it's natural that you may be hesitant to expose yourself to further vulnerability. *Are you worried that showing compassion will leave you vulnerable?*

- **Lack of awareness or denial:** You may cope with your painful experiences by minimizing or denying the impact of your parents' actions. It could, therefore, be challenging for you to feel compassion and face the reality of the hurt you suffered. *Could this be why the thought of being compassionate is so hard to deal with?*

These are all rational responses to pain and suffering, so you're not unusual in that respect. However, your story is unique, and self-healing is a gradual process that takes time. There is no rush to race toward a position of compassion for your parents if you don't feel ready. It may help to consider how beneficial it will be for you to get to a point in life where all of the pain, fear, grief, and shame melts away.

To further explore the process of extending compassion to a parent, let's take a look through the eyes of Sarah, a 30-year-old woman who had a challenging relationship with her father during her teenage years. Sarah's father was often absent due to his work commitments, and when he was around, he struggled to connect with her on an emotional level. This left Sarah feeling neglected and unimportant.

Years later, the adult Sarah reflected on her upbringing and realized the impact it had on her self-esteem and relationships. She decided to work toward extending compassion and forgiveness to her father.

- Sarah began by **reflecting on her father's perspective**. She realized that his demanding job required long hours and that he was under a lot of pressure to provide for the family. This reflection helped Sarah understand the challenges her father was facing.

- She then **put herself in her father's shoes**, imagining the stress he must have felt while trying to balance work and family responsibilities. She considered the possibility that he might not have known how to express love and support in the way she needed.

- Sarah **recognized that her father was human**, with flaws and limitations, just like everyone else. After acknowledging this, it was easier for her to understand that her father had made mistakes and faced his own set of struggles.

- She **sought common ground,** identifying shared experiences from her childhood, such as family outings or special moments spent together. By focusing on positive memories, she was able to build a connection that made it easier for her to view her father with compassion.

- Sarah **decided to have an open and honest conversation** with her father. She shared her feelings from her teenage years and expressed how neglected she'd felt. She also told him about the impact his actions had on her and expressed her desire for understanding and healing.

- Then, she **established boundaries** in her current relationships, making it clear what behaviors were unacceptable to her. This helped create a safe space for compassion without exposing her to ongoing emotional harm.

- Sarah also began **engaging in mindfulness practices** to stay present during her interactions with her father. This helped her manage emotions as they emerged and allowed her to respond to the situation calmly.

- She started to **practice forgiveness meditation**, which involved visualizing moments of connection with her father and cultivating feelings of compassion and understanding.

- Sarah now **consciously turns her focus to her father's positive qualities**, such as his strong work ethic, determination, and desire to support his family. This has helped her to reframe her perspective and find a healthier sense of balance.

Although your situation will be different than Sarah's, these strategies can be adapted to suit your unique case if you wish to extend compassion to your parents. Through the process, you may understand more about them and eventually find it easier to forgive. You have nothing to lose and everything to gain by trying.

Adopting a forgiving mindset

It can be easier to understand forgiveness once you understand the practice of compassion. When you adopt self-compassion, you'll more likely be able to acknowledge and feel the suffering of others. You may understand that someone hurt you because they were experiencing pain. Once you recognize this, you'll experience a sense of softening, understanding, and release.

This was certainly the case in my relationship with my father. Once I reached a place where I could view him with compassion, it became obvious to me that he must have been a very unhappy man. No doubt he had his own struggles to cope with and, unfortunately, he wasn't able to develop any kind of self-awareness or reflect on his harmful actions toward his family. Still, over time, I was able to extend compassion to him on a human level, easing the negative emotions I used to hold in my heart. This led me to have a forgiving mindset, making me more able to forgive myself and others for any flaws, weaknesses, mistakes, or imperfections.

When we forgive someone who has wronged us, we transfer the pain of what happened to a state of recovery by managing our emotions. At the helm of those emotions is the mind—our hard drive. Forgiveness should therefore be seen as a mental process, not a one-off event. The more we practice forgiveness, the more we build a habit, enabling our minds to rewire and form new neural connections.[42]

You can adopt a forgiving mindset by using the following strategies:

- Learn to be aware of how you feel mentally and physically when thinking about past experiences. *Do you feel anger, frustration, fear, or any other emotions?*

- Notice the changes in your body as you respond to pain. *Do you feel tense, sweaty, shaky, or uncomfortable?*

- Consider writing down your reflections to help organize your thinking and give yourself more clarity. *How can you disconnect from the pain through forgiveness?*

- Practice seeing pain differently to disempower it and change the way it affects your well-being. Then, imagine forgiving the people who harmed you.

- Try stating forgiveness out loud. This could sound something like this:

    - "I forgive x for y."

    - "I understand that they acted from a place of pain."

    - "I will no longer be affected by what they did to me."

Through these simple steps, you can release deeply entrenched emotions. Your focus will turn from pain to healing, allowing you to adopt a mindset that is more capable of forgiving others.

Finally, remind yourself every day that you are in control of how you react to events in life. You have the power to create your own story and craft your own happy ending.

Reflection

- *What kinds of things do you beat yourself up about?*
- *How do you feel after you have scorned yourself and been self-critical?*
- *What positive emotions do you experience when you show compassion for others?*
- *How often do you practice self-kindness? What is stopping you from practicing it more often?*
- *How often do you experience painful emotions that remind you of your childhood?*
- *In which ways would you like to begin extending compassion to your parents?*
- *Do you find the idea of disconnecting from your pain through forgiveness challenging?*

In the next chapter, we'll explore the five steps to forgiveness and learn how to sail stormy seas on our journey to find the peace we long for. But first, take a moment to reflect on what you have gained thus far and ask yourself, "Am I any nearer to being able to forgive my parents?" Hopefully, you're getting closer to considering the possibility and are ready to move on to the next stage.

Chapter 7

The Process of Forgiveness

"Forgiveness is not an occasional act; it is a constant attitude."
—Martin Luther King Jr.

WHAT'S YOUR MOTIVATION FOR wanting to forgive your parents?

Perhaps you just want to "do the right thing" on a personal level. Maybe knowing that forgiveness is beneficial for your physical, mental, and emotional health—in addition to improving your relationships with others—makes it seems like a worthwhile pursuit.

You might have religious motives for forgiving, with your faith extolling the virtues of forgiveness as a way to come closer to God. Your spiritual beliefs might drive you to find inner peace, of which forgiving others plays a crucial role. Similarly, cultural pressures could make you want to follow the societal norms of being seen as a nice, kind, forgiving person.[43]

There may be multiple reasons you wish to forgive. We're all complicated human beings living in a complex world, and we're all motivated by a myriad of reasons. Yet, studies show that when people forgive for external reasons, they don't experience the same depth of forgiveness as when they're motivated by a deeper, altruistic love. This is a great challenge for most of us, especially after suffering at the hands of somebody as important as a parent.

Many real-life cases showcase forgiveness under seemingly unthinkable conditions. Mothers have forgiven their children's murderers, victims of hate crimes have forgiven their perpetrators, and those imprisoned have forgiven their torturers.

In one example, the 2013 movie "The Railway Man" depicts the true story of Eric Lomax, a British Army Officer who was captured by the Japanese during World War II and forced to work on the construction of the Thai-Burma Railway, famously known as the "Death Railway." Lomax struggles to come to terms with the forced labor and torture he endured while being held as a prisoner of war, unable to overcome the severe psychological trauma resulting from his wartime experiences. He becomes so obsessed with vengeance that he sets out to find and confront one of his captors, Takashi Nagase.

As the story unfolds, "The Railway Man" delves into themes of reconciliation and the impact of trauma on individuals and relationships. It's a poignant exploration of the human capacity for forgiveness and the long-lasting consequences of wartime experiences. As with many similar stories about forgiveness, the main character finally finds peace and closure decades after his terrible ordeal.

When such stories are put into context, forgiving your parents for their perceived wrongs might seem more feasible. While the harm you endured is still very real and valid, forgiveness is possible even in the most extreme cases.

The five steps to forgiveness: the REACH model

The REACH model for forgiveness was introduced by clinical psychologist Everett L. Worthington Jr. in his book, "Five Steps to Forgiveness: The Art and Science of Forgiving" (Crown Publishers, 2003).[44] It describes two levels of forgiveness: decisional and emotional. The first level, decisional forgiveness, involves deciding to let go of angry and resentful thoughts or feelings. Emotional forgiveness then takes this a step further by replacing the negative emotions with positive feelings like compassion, sympathy, and empathy.

REACH is an acronym for:

Recall—remembering hurt as objectively as you can.

Empathize—trying to understand the viewpoint of the person who wronged you.

Altruistic Gift—thinking about a time you hurt someone and were forgiven, and then offering the gift of forgiveness to the person who hurt you.

Committing—publicly forgiving the person who wronged you.

Holding on—not forgetting hurt, but reminding yourself that you made the choice to forgive.

Next, we'll take a closer look at each step, with examples to show how the REACH model for forgiveness can be applied:

1. **Recall**

    - This step involves revisiting the details of hurtful events. It's best to do this when you're in a calm state of mind rather than when you feel agitated, upset, or angry. When you're able, take time to reflect on what happened, how you felt, and the impact it had on you. In this first step, the aim isn't to dwell on the negative but to acknowledge and understand your feelings.

    - For example, if a parent humiliated you by scorning you in front of your friends, you could recall the specific incident and the emotions you experienced, such as betrayal, anger, or sadness.

2. **Empathize**

    - In this step, the goal is to understand the perspective of the person who caused you the harm. Rather than excusing or justifying their actions, you're trying to gain insight into their motivations or circumstances.

    - Empathizing with a parent might involve considering factors such as their own insecurities, upbringing, or struggles that may have contributed to their behavior. Through this step, you can foster a broader understanding of the situation.

3. **Altruistic Gift**

    - Offering the gift of forgiveness is the key aspect of this step. Here, you need to make a conscious decision to let go of resentment and the desire for revenge. Instead, you choose to forgive for your own well-being.

    - Offering altruistic gift to your parents may involve recognizing that holding onto anger and resentment is harming your own mental and emotional health. By forgiving them, you're releasing the heavy burden of those negative emotions. Altruism involves showing a genuine concern for the well-being of others, but it's also a healing remedy for your own pain.

4. **Commit**

    - Make a conscious decision to maintain the stance of forgiveness you've granted. By fully committing to forgiveness, you can navigate the obstacles of the process much easier.

    - To do so, you may choose not to bring up past harm in future conflicts with your parents, and you might avoid dwelling on negative thoughts related to their offenses.

Here, you're committing to an ongoing process of healing. Writing a simple note to yourself can help. Simply state, "Today, I forgave [person's name]."

5. **Hold On**

    ○ The final, and perhaps most demanding, step involves maintaining forgiveness over time. This will require you to deal with lingering negative emotions that arise and actively work on sustaining forgiveness.

    ○ Instead of allowing past grievances to resurface and impact your current relationship with your parents, hold onto forgiveness and begin the process of letting go and moving forward.

While these steps are not one-size-fits-all, they can act as a guide as you steer a course toward forgiveness. Your personal journey comes with its unique challenges and perspectives, but it's worth noting that forgiveness can be achieved, both on a decisional and emotional level.[45]

From blame to empowerment

When we suffer a harmful experience at the hands of someone else, we experience what's known as an "injustice gap." This is an ongoing mental computation in which we balance the amount of injustice done to us with subsequent events related to the transgression.[46]

For example, your parents might make things seem more unjust by continuing hurtful behavior that shows no sign of ending. This can make the injustice gap even larger. On the other hand, they might behave in such a way that some sense of justice is restored when you think about the offense. If they apologize sincerely or try to make amends in other ways, for instance, the injustice gap can narrow.

The difficulty of forgiving is, therefore, directly related to the size of the injustice gap. At the same time, the "blame game" doesn't bring you anything constructive but rather keeps you locked in a cycle of negative thinking. It's a type of victim attitude that gives too much power to others and prevents you from taking control of your life.

To reduce this gap and feel more empowered, you'll need to combine your cognitive and emotional skills. If, for instance, you're struggling with parents who didn't give you the emotional support you needed when you were younger, you may need to change the way you view the past to allow yourself to gradually gain a more balanced view. As you reflect on perceived injustice, you can consider if your interpretation is valid or accurate.[47]

Remember that whatever you have felt up until now is valid, and this process isn't about negating those emotions. But perhaps you can explore alternative perspectives that will allow you to understand the situation more objectively:

- You might try to see things from both sides, considering other viewpoints. When you do so, it's more possible to foster empathy and gain a contextual understanding of the perceived injustice that occurred.

- You can try to differentiate between facts and your interpretations of them. Sometimes, our emotional response to a situation is based more on our interpretation of events than on actual facts. Generally, our childhood worldviews don't perfectly align with the ways we see things through adult eyes. Is it possible that the facts as you remember them are not a true representation of what occurred, or that your interpretation of them needs rethinking?

- A useful exercise is to challenge your thoughts about perceived injustice. Ask yourself if your thoughts are based on evidence or assumptions. Were your parents really as unsupportive as you remember, or were your expectations of them too high? Maybe they were incapable of meeting your needs. Recognizing this can lead toward reducing the blame you apportion to them.

- What's done is done, although the pain and hurt can linger for a lifetime. This is why it's so important for you to focus on what you can control now. You have no control over the past or how others behave in your present, but taking the reins can give you an incredible sense of empowerment. This ultimately leads to less feelings of helplessness and a more positive outlook on life.

- Your personal growth is a priority, so use your experience as an opportunity to learn and mature. What lessons can you take from the situation? What strengths can you cultivate to become more resilient? By investing time and energy in yourself, you can gain a liberating sense of empowerment and also help to nurture your personal development and well-being.

- You can practice mindfulness techniques to stay focused on the present—accepting the current situation without excessive judgment. As previously mentioned, acceptance doesn't mean condoning the injustice, but rather acknowledging it and choosing how to respond.

- You may find it beneficial to cultivate gratitude by focusing on aspects of your life you are grateful for. In doing so, your attention will shift from perceived injustices to an appreciation of all the good things you have. Rather than thinking about the wrongs done to you, reflect on all the rights in your life and give thanks for those.

- You can make a decision to forgive, not for the person who did you wrong, but for yourself. When you release the hold that negative emotions have on you, you'll begin to develop a growth mindset full of positivity.

Celebrating progress

Believe it or not, one day in the calendar year has been attributed to forgiving. Global Forgiveness Day is observed annually on July 7th. First established in 1994, it gained popularity throughout the world as a time to practice forgiving others and ourselves. Although forgiveness is a daily work in progress, having a specific date marked on your calendar may remind you of where you are on your journey and provide an opportunity for you to celebrate how far you've come.

But, of course, you don't have to wait until July 7th to celebrate any small wins. You can do so daily by acknowledging the progress you have made and by recognizing when you chose empowerment over blame. Each small step you take is a building block on the road to personal development and liberation from past pain.

Some ways to celebrate your progress include:

- **Celebrate small milestones.** Break down your forgiveness journey into smaller milestones and celebrate each achievement. Did you go a week without dwelling on the past or enjoy a day of inner peace? Acknowledge your accomplishment and give yourself a pat on the back (or choose another small reward).

- **Practice self-care.** Treat yourself by engaging in activities that promote self-care and well-being. You could choose to indulge in a new hobby, take a day off work, or simply spend time doing something you really enjoy.

- **Express gratitude.** This is a wonderful way to acknowledge all of the positive changes and healing you've gone through. As explored in chapter three, you can give thanks for your life, friends, family, or others who have helped you on your journey.

- **Create a ritual or ceremony.** Light a candle, write yourself a letter, or even write a letter to the person you forgave (you don't need to send it). Any symbolic gesture you can think of represents your journey toward forgiveness and will instill you with greater inner peace.

- **Watch a movie about forgiveness.** Let yourself get inspired by the stories of others. Some options are:

    - Invictus, 2009: This biographical sports drama features Matt Damon and Morgan Freeman. It's based on the true story of a rugby team affected by apartheid in the mid-1990s.

    - Lady Bird, 2014: This drama revolves around a young girl, played by Saoirse Ronan, who longs to flee from her family. Her final year of high school ultimately leads to a process of healing and forgiveness.

    - Jojo Rabbit, 2019: This satirical movie revolves around a young boy in Nazi Germany who discovers that his mother is hiding a Jewish girl in their home. It explores themes of love, compassion, and forgiveness in the face of prejudice and hatred.

    - Philomena, 2013: This is a powerful story about a political journalist who follows a woman's search for her son. Judy Dench plays Philomena, determined to find out what happened to her newborn after he was taken away from her decades earlier by convent nuns. The movie explores the power of forgiveness and acceptance.

- **Acknowledge your growth.** As you learn to master your own life, free from the constraints of your past, take time to celebrate. Look at yourself in the mirror and see the reflection of someone with resilience and strength instead of the bitter, resentful person you used to be.

- **Set new goals.** Write a commitment statement to yourself, noting what you wish to accomplish and how you can achieve it. Use it as a mission statement to bring even more positive changes into your life.

- **Share your achievements.** Being able to talk about your past can bring a lighter heart. Share your journey with a close friend, family member, or therapist, and talk about the significance of your progress.

- If it fits your situation, you may choose to **reach out to your perceived wrongdoer and let them know you have forgiven them.** Make sure not to do this with the expectation that they'll respond in the way you'd like, if at all. Instead, do it as a celebration of your emotional freedom from past pain and as recognition of your self-healing.

- **Share your forgiveness story more widely**, perhaps through a blog or social media post. When you share your experiences, you may inspire others to forgive the people in their lives.

- **Teach the importance of forgiveness.** If you have children of your own—or if you have nephews, nieces, or other youngsters in your circle—you can teach them the same skills of forgiveness that you've acquired. You can spare children a lot of pain by showing them how to forgive from an early age. With older children or other adults, you can talk about the importance of forgiveness for their emotional and physical health.

When you can acknowledge your progress, express self-compassion, and reinforce positive behaviors that contribute to your overall well-being, you'll be motivated to continue on the path toward forgiveness and personal growth.

Reflection

- *What past experiences could you perceive differently?*
- *How do those experiences affect the size of the "injustice gap" you feel?*
- *How do you think you could be more forgiving?*
- *Are there any negative emotions toward someone who hurt you that you can let go of?*
- *Who do you respect for their ability to forgive?*
- *How will you go about celebrating your progress on the road to forgiveness?*

As you become more forgiving, you may find yourself ready to rebuild relationships with those who hurt you in the past—although this is never a requirement of forgiveness. In the next chapter, we'll explore strategies to help open the lines of communication and nurture positive connections, should you choose to do so.

Chapter 8

Rebuilding Relationships

"If there is to be reconciliation, first there must be truth."
—Timothy B. Tyson

THERE'S NO GOING BACK to the past or erasing painful events—what's done is done. Similarly, you cannot change your parents or their behavior. Even if you manage to forgive them, you may not want them to be a part of your life going forward.

This is understandable and valid, especially if they continue to trigger you, cross boundaries, or treat you poorly. Through your gradual process of recentering and emotional healing, you may have decided it is better not to try to rebuild any kind of relationship with them. If you feel at peace with this choice, you do not need to feel pressured to change it.

Conversely, perhaps you feel there is some value in reconnecting, and you would like to explore the idea of reconciliation with your parents. At this point, it's important to recognize that your aim shouldn't be to try to "fix" what is broken—that's not your job. As a child, you had no say over how you were treated, and it wasn't a level playing field. The adults in your life had the power and authority while you were—in large part—helpless. Now that you are older, you are responsible for your own actions, but that doesn't mean you should feel obliged to mend broken fences.

Rebuilding a relationship after forgiveness is a transformative process that transcends trying to patch up old wounds. It is about creating something new—forming a connection based on a different playing field. Now, you stand as an empowered and autonomous individual, no longer burdened by guilt or shame tied to your parents' behavior. You have come to understand that their actions do not define you or dictate your future.

This newfound clarity and self-assurance will allow you to consider rebuilding the relationship from a position of strength, not weakness. Since you no longer feel the need to appease or seek validation from those who once caused you pain, you can assert your right to be treated with dignity and respect.

- This shift in perspective allows you to set healthier boundaries and communicate your needs effectively.

- You understand that reconciliation does not mean surrendering your autonomy or sacrificing your well-being for the sake of appeasing others.

- You recognize that true reconciliation can only occur when both parties are committed to mutual growth and understanding.

It is possible you will encounter setbacks and challenges along the way. You may recognize old patterns of behavior resurfacing or feel triggered by familiar actions. But you can now stand firm in the knowledge that you are deserving of love and compassion.

Most notably, rebuilding a relationship after forgiveness is not about erasing the past or pretending that the hurt never happened. It's about acknowledging the pain, embracing the lessons learned, and moving forward with courage and resilience.

Reconciliation after forgiveness is about reclaiming your power and creating a future filled with hope, healing, and the possibility of genuine connection.

While the root of your relationship with your parents may appear rotten, you can plant new seeds that may grow into a flourishing future with them in it. And most importantly, you get to dictate the terms of the new relationship—ensuring prioritization of your boundaries and needs.

So, why consider reestablishing a connection? Research shows that building healthy bonds with family has many positive outcomes, including the following:

- **Improved mental health**: When your family relationships are healthy, you are likely to experience lower levels of stress, anxiety, and depression.[48] Additionally, research shows that having a supportive family environment—including positive relationships with parents—is associated with a decreased risk of developing mental health disorders.[49]

- **Enhanced emotional well-being**: Reestablishing a connection with your parents may provide emotional support, reduce feelings of loneliness, and contribute to your overall sense of belonging.[50]

- **Increased resilience**: Rebuilding relationships with parents can contribute to the development of resilience and mental strength. Resilience enables you to cope more effectively with life's challenges and bounce back from adversity.[51]

- **Enhanced physical health**: Having a strong family support system can lead to lower blood pressure, improved immune function, and a reduced risk of chronic illnesses.[52]

- **Longer life expectancy**: Research shows that individuals with strong social connections—including family ties—tend to live longer. This could be because the stress of isolation can weaken people's immune systems, making them more susceptible to infectious diseases. If you have strong social connections, you are also more likely to engage in better health behaviors such as eating better and being more physically active.[53]

- **Better coping skills**: Reestablishing a relationship with your parents can provide you with additional resources and support for coping with challenges in life.[54]

- **Higher levels of happiness**: Studies have found a positive correlation between strong family relationships and higher levels of happiness and life satisfaction.[55]

While you no doubt would like to experience these benefits, you must also acknowledge that your relationship with your parents is based on specific circumstances. They must also be willing to actively participate in the rebuilding process. In the event that they are averse to this, or if they are no longer around, reconciliation may simply not be possible. If this applies to your situation, the most helpful path you can take is accepting your reality and focusing on other avenues to create positive change in your life.

However, if you find yourself in a place where you think that reestablishing a relationship with your parents may be possible and worth pursuing, the rest of this chapter will outline strategies to help you in this endeavor.

Opening the lines of communication

The first step toward reconciliation can be the hardest. *How do you make the first move? What do you say? What will their reaction be? How can you prepare for possible rejection?*

Setting a plan prior to trying to open the lines of communication can help set you up for the best chances of success:

- Consider your intentions:
    - Why do you want to reconnect?
    - What do you hope to achieve?
- Try to choose the right time:
    - Find a time when both parties are likely to be in a calm and receptive state of mind.
    - Avoid reaching out during significant family events or emotionally charged moments.
- Use technology, if it is accessible:
    - Messaging, emails, video calls, or phone conversations can initiate a connection without the pressure of a physical meeting.
    - However, stay mindful of the fact that tones—especially subtle ones like sarcasm—can easily be misinterpreted through digital communication.
- Write a letter:
    - Writing allows you to more thoroughly plan what you want to say to ensure you accurately express your thoughts.
    - Reaching out via written communication also gives your parents time to digest what you have said before responding.
- Tell them you want to reconcile:
    - Be clear about your desire for reconciliation and rebuilding the relationship.

- Share that you are open to finding common ground and moving forward together.

- Be honest about how you feel:
  - It's best to be honest about your feelings from the offset.
  - You should also show your willingness to listen to their perspective.
  - Avoid blaming; use "I" statements to convey your emotions and experiences.

- Acknowledge past issues:
  - Refer to past issues or conflicts without apportioning blame.
  - Describe your feelings and experiences in a neutral way.
  - Emphasize that you are interested in moving beyond past challenges.

- Set clear boundaries:
  - Define clear boundaries and expectations at the beginning.
  - This will provide a base on which to build respect and understanding.

- Try to prepare yourself for their reactions:
  - Understand that your parents may react differently than the way you expect or hope.
  - Be prepared for a range of responses and remain as patient as you can.

- Meet in a neutral setting:

    - If you opt for a physical meeting, public places typically work best. This could be a quiet café or a public park.

    - You could also arrange to meet via a mediator, depending on the circumstances.

- Seek professional guidance as needed:

    - If the estrangement has been prolonged or involves complex issues, you may consider seeking the guidance of a family therapist or counselor.

    - A neutral third party can help facilitate communication and address underlying issues.

Reopening communication is a gradual process that requires the willingness of both parties. As such, progress can take time. With patience and a genuine desire to reconnect, it is possible to build bridges in many scenarios.

Establishing trust

How do you trust someone who has hurt you in the past? This can be incredibly difficult, and even more so if you haven't completely overcome trauma or if you are still unsure about approaching your perceived wrongdoers.

Perhaps you have been estranged from your parents for so long that you have no idea if efforts to reestablish some kind of relationship will bear fruit. *Will they live up to their word or hurt you again?*

If you have gone through the process of deep healing, you are likely in a place where you have separated the past from the present. Since you are an autonomous individual, you can now reclaim your power and agency. In essence, you are not the same person you were before and are, therefore, you are not capable of being hurt in the same way. This means that you have less to fear as you make the move toward attempting reconciliation with your parents. Since mistrust is often based on fear, hopefully, you will be able to stretch out an olive branch without being afraid of the negative consequences it could have on your emotional balance.

Trust is a vital part of any relationship. Without it, the chances of building healthy connections are slim. You may want to first consider if you trust yourself enough.

- Are you prepared to be open, vulnerable, and honest with your parents?

- Have you done enough self-work to trust in your ability to remain neutral and dispassionate?

- Do you have a clear sense of what your boundaries are, and can you recognize when they are being encroached upon?

- Can you communicate your feelings and thoughts effectively?

- Are you prepared to respect and understand your parents' needs?

- Do you trust yourself to respond to any challenges with a calm mind and a peaceful heart?

Since you cannot know for sure how your parents will react or behave as you approach them, all you can do is control your own behavior to foster trust. The following guidelines can help with this process:

- **Be honest and transparent**: Openness and honesty about your thoughts, feelings, and intentions are necessary if you want to start rebuilding trust. You must be prepared to lay yourself on the line without holding back.

- **Turn your words into action**: It's important to walk the talk, which means keeping your promises, sticking to plans, and being consistent in your actions. This will help to build trust over time.

- **Respect *their* boundaries**: Just as you should expect your parents to respect your limitations, you should be prepared to respect theirs. For example, you cannot demand that they reestablish a relationship with you just because you desire it.

- **Be prepared to listen**: If your parents have something to say, listen to them, acknowledge their perspectives, and show empathy. Even if you don't agree, actively listening can help build mutual respect and trust.

- **Apologize when necessary**: If you played a part in the breakdown of the relationship, a sincere apology may be needed. Acknowledging any mistakes you've made can go a long way in rebuilding trust.

- **Show patience and understanding**: It may be difficult for your parents to enter into a new relationship with you, so you may need to allow them time to process. Trust isn't gained overnight, and they may not be in the right place to move forward yet.

- **Focus on building positive memories**: Instead of bringing up the past, try to create opportunities to build positive memories together. Do activities you both enjoy and create new experiences that strengthen your bond and build trust.

Exploring reconciliation scenarios

Imagine that you and your parents have finally agreed to meet and discuss your relationship over coffee.

During the conversation, your parents seem hesitant about committing to reestablishing ties, and they express that they aren't sure what you expect of them. The most helpful thing you can do is to listen to them, acknowledge their feelings, and explain your position with honesty and transparency. Tell them you are willing to reconcile under certain conditions and clearly lay out your boundaries. Don't expect a relationship to blossom immediately, but rather view this as a first step on the way to possible reconciliation.

You may reach a point where you have established a reasonably decent relationship with your parents but haven't quite fully bridged the gap. This can be a healthy and realistic outcome given the complexities of your past. Even with unresolved feelings on both sides, if you are mutually able to set and respect boundaries, it is possible to foster a limited but pleasant relationship. Depending on your situation, this may include allowing your parents to spend time with their grandchildren.

For instance, consider Javier, a single father. After being estranged from his parents for years due to unresolved conflicts stemming from his teenage years, Javier decided to reconnect with them in adulthood. They managed to rebuild a civil and respectful relationship through open communication and mutual efforts to understand each other's perspectives. While Javier and his parents made significant progress in addressing past issues, a lingering emotional distance prevented them from getting closer.

Despite this, both Javier and his parents are grateful to have reached a point of mutual acceptance and understanding. They've agreed to disagree on certain matters and have established ground rules to ensure that conflicts are managed respectfully. While there may still be unresolved feelings simmering beneath the surface, they've learned to navigate these complexities with maturity.

Javier finds it easier to maintain the relationship with his parents through their interactions with his two sons. He sees positivity stemming from his children's relationship with their grandparents, and all boundaries have been respected.

While they may never become an idyllic close-knit family, Javier is content with the fact that they've found a way to get along and respect each other's boundaries and priorities. Setting both realistic expectations and clear boundaries early on was key to fostering mutual respect. As a result, Javier has actually been surprised at how well his parents and his sons have been able to bond.

Nurturing positive connections

Once you have set the wheels in motion and established some kind of new relationship with your parents, you will need to remain mindful of the situation moving forward. For the new connection to flourish and grow, it will be necessary to consistently put in the right amount of time and energy.

If meetings with your parents don't enrich the relationship or help deepen the bond, they will soon begin to feel like a waste of time. It is helpful to consider ways of nurturing a more positive connection. This is where the concept of "minding" comes in.

First presented in 1997, the theory of **minding** is now seen as an essential tool for maintaining close and satisfying relationships.[56] Although the initial minding theory referred more to couples, it can be adapted to the adult child-parent dynamic. In a well-minded relationship, one would expect to find a mixture of equality, empathy, negotiation, companionship, and deep commitment. This may seem like an ambitious goal to achieve as you rebuild a relationship with your parents, but moving in this direction is helpful.

The five components of minding are:

1. **Revealing your true self and actively listening**:

    - Being prepared to disclose information about yourself can help develop a sense of self-worth, cognitive processing, feelings of closeness, and intimacy.

    - When both parties have mutual knowledge of each other, greater closeness can be fostered.

    - While it is understandable that you may not want to share all details of your life with your parents, perhaps you consider telling them about what you love to do or how you feel about certain world events.

2. **Seeing positive attributions**:

    - Perceiving your parents as having good intent and attributing negative events to situational or unintentional causes can help to build a healthy relationship.

    - This outlook can promote greater emotional well-being and help you to see your parents in a more positive light.

3. **Accepting and respecting anything shared with you**:

    - Be prepared to show acceptance, support, and respect when your parents share information with you.

    - This will lead to greater closeness as you put things into perspective and don't feel the need to judge or condemn their past actions.

4. **Reciprocating thoughts, feelings, and behaviors**:

    - By reciprocating your parents' thoughts and showing empathy, you are demonstrating your willingness to improve your relationship with them.

- Caring about others and their welfare has enormous benefits, as long as it does not compromise your values or well-being.

5. **Continuing to process and invest in the relationship**:

    - Even when things aren't going perfectly, staying optimistic and maintaining control of yourself within the relationship will create a sense of unity over time.

    - As the bond becomes stronger, it will get easier to manage the ups and downs while staying supportive.

If, despite your best efforts, you determine that the relationship isn't going to be revived, renewed, or refreshed, then it may be best to leave things as they are. Regardless of how much you may want to build a healthy parent-child bond, it may simply not be possible. Your parents may be unwilling or incapable of making the changes needed. While you may end up feeling like your efforts for reconciliation were a waste of time, try not to regret going through the process, as it can still serve as a valuable growth experience for you. And remember: it is not a reflection of you if your parents cannot or will not meet you halfway.

If you feel frustrated that you were unable to find the closure you hoped for, recognize that closure comes from within you. You will need to move forward with your life and accept that some relationships will never be fully mended. While reconciliation may be an elusive pursuit, you will come to realize that the ability to liberate yourself from past pain was always in your own hands.

You can find solace in the knowledge that you hold the key to your own healing and liberation—through self-awareness, strength, and acceptance.

Reflection

- *If you plan to attempt to reestablish a relationship with your parents, what do you hope to gain from this pursuit?*

- *What aspects of your life do you feel will benefit from rebuilding a parent-child relationship?*

- *How can you best prepare to approach your parents?*

- *What response do you expect them to have about your reaching out?*

- *How will you respond if your efforts to reestablish a connection fail?*

- *How can you nurture trust in your potential new relationship with your parents?*

- *How do you envision a healthier relationship with your parents in the future?*

As you continue through life, you may not recognize all of the ways in which your prior trauma continues to impact your decisions. What happens if you find yourself in the role of parent yourself? How do you deal with negative patterns of learned behavior that may emerge? The next chapter will explore these concepts and provide strategies for dealing with anxiety about your parenting capabilities through emotional intelligence and mindfulness.

CHAPTER 9

BREAKING THE CYCLE

"Identifying the pattern is awareness; choosing not to repeat the cycle is growth."

—Billy Chapata

MOST OF OUR THOUGHTS and feelings are learned responses to what we have experienced in life. Similarly, our behavior is generally based on emotion, and it doesn't necessarily reflect our true character.

For example, imagine getting stopped by highway patrol on your daily commute to work. Do you immediately feel guilty for having done something wrong? Does the uniformed officer terrify you? Do you feel angry and unjustly targeted? When the officer tells you that you have a faulty taillight, do you tremble, apologize profusely, or get agitated? The way you react is an outward expression of how you have learned to behave when under stress.

Social learning theory ("SLT"), first introduced by social psychologist Albert Bandura in the 1960s, explains that we observe, model, and imitate the emotional reactions, attitudes, and behaviors of others in learning.[57] Bandura's ideas later developed into the social cognitive theory, which posits that learning takes place in a social context, "with a dynamic and reciprocal interaction of the person, environment, and behavior, and a cognitive context that considers past experiences that shape engagement in behavior."[58]

Breaking this down into simpler terms—we learn through direct reinforcement and punishment, as well as by observing the actions of others and the consequences of those actions. The example of Bandura's famous inflatable Bobo doll illustrates this perfectly. In this study, a group of children observed an adult model behaving aggressively toward a doll. They were then placed into a room with the same doll while their behavior was observed. A second group of children were placed with the doll without observing the aggressive behavior.

Not surprisingly, the children who observed the aggressive model were more likely to imitate that aggressive behavior toward the Bobo doll than the children who hadn't observed the model. The study showed that what we see can influence our behavior, even when no punishment or enforcement is present.

Our concept of self-efficacy also factors into how our behavior is shaped. Self-efficacy is our belief in our ability to successfully perform a specific task or behavior. Bandura proposed that these beliefs in self-efficacy influence the choices we make, our level of effort, and our persistence in the face of obstacles. This can be seen across various domains, such as academic, sporting, and career performance. It also extends to how successful we are at maintaining close relationships.

In summation, Bandura's SLT provided evidence that our thoughts, feelings, and behaviors are influenced by our experiences, observations of others, and our beliefs about our capabilities. Today, behavioral psychology, cognitive-behavioral therapy, and SLT point to how these experiences affect us in the following ways:

- **Cognitive conditioning:** Our thoughts and beliefs are often shaped by our upbringing, experiences, and environment. For example, if you consistently received positive reinforcement for getting good grades in school while growing up, you are more likely to have developed positive thoughts and beliefs about the importance of schoolwork. By contrast, receiving negative reinforcement will have a knock-on effect on the way you think and feel about those behaviors now.

- **Emotional conditioning**: Our feelings and emotional responses can be influenced by past experiences and learned associations. For instance, if you have had negative experiences with your parents, you may notice an involuntary response of fear or anxiety when faced with similar circumstances.

- **Behavioral conditioning**: Our actions and behaviors are often learned through reinforcement, punishment, and observation of others. For example, if you were rewarded for a particular behavior, you may be more inclined to adopt that behavior in the future. On the other hand, if you were punished for something you did, you may avoid repeating the action later in life.

- **Social learning:** We learn from the behaviors and experiences of those around us, such as family members, peers, and cultural influences. Our behavior can also be influenced by role models, societal norms, and expectations. Such experiences influence our thoughts, feelings, and behaviors—although it's important to note that they may not always reflect your true character or values.

Breaking the cycle of how you respond to your parents' wrongdoings—rather than allowing yourself to be a prisoner of your past—requires a lot of self-awareness, reflection, and intentional effort. Consciously aligning your true values and beliefs to your feelings and thoughts is an ongoing process that occurs over time as you mature.

Balancing responsibility and forgiveness

Achieving a balance between responsibility and forgiveness is complex. It involves acknowledging accountability for your actions while also extending compassion and understanding to yourself and others. When you find yourself reacting to situations negatively, you are likely responding to a learned pattern of behavior.

For instance, when your partner yells at you, you may shut down instead of defending yourself. If you feel angry about something that happened at work, you might take it out on your kids by snapping at them. Of course, you may regret your response minutes later, but in the moment, you are mimicking learned behavior. These types of behaviors have become so familiar that you believe that they define your character.

To break such negative patterns of emotions, feelings, and actions, you have to do the hard work of understanding how these patterns were learned in the first place. Next, you will need to forgive yourself for not being able to react in any other way when you were younger. After that, it's important to acknowledge that you are now responsible for your behavior and admit that you seek self-growth for a better future.

Reaching the point where you are able to break the cycle of learned emotional responses requires balance. The following "BALANCE" acronym lays out steps you can take to achieve that. These don't need to be followed in any particular order, but gradually working toward incorporating all of them will help to bring you the most benefit.

BALANCE

B—Boundaries

A—Accountability

L—Let go

A—Apologize and make amends

N—Nurture empathy

C—Compassion

E—Embrace growth and change

Boundaries: As previously established, boundaries help to define expectations and create a sense of safety and respect in relationships. Take time to thoughtfully set your limits and then communicate them with assertiveness and clarity.

Accountability: As an adult, you should be able to hold yourself and others accountable for actions in a constructive and non-judgmental manner. If you are trying to mend fences with your parents, for example, it is easier to reestablish the relationship if you show accountability to foster trust, integrity, and growth.

Let go of resentment: The longer you hold onto grudges, the more persistent the negativity becomes. To heal and move forward, you have to be prepared to let go of the burden of past hurts.

Apologize and make amends: When you recognize that you are causing harm or hurt to others, offer a sincere apology and make amends. It takes maturity to acknowledge your mistakes, express remorse, and take corrective action to repair the damage done, but the benefits are vast.

Nurture empathy: When you make the effort to understand the perspectives and experiences of others, you can better appreciate the complexities of human behavior. Fostering forgiveness toward anyone who has done you a perceived wrong will then become second nature.

Compassion: By understanding that everyone makes mistakes and no one is perfect, you will learn to grow without being overly self-critical of your faults.

Embrace growth and change: Achieving this harmony is an ongoing journey that requires patience, self-awareness, and a willingness to learn and adapt. Be kind to yourself and look ahead, not back.

Integrating these principles into your life and cultivating a balanced approach to responsibility and forgiveness promotes healing, growth, and positive relationships with yourself and others.

Applying lessons from your journey

If you end up having children of your own, you will likely find it to be one of the biggest tests of your life (albeit one of the most rewarding). *How do you prevent your chronic feelings of anger toward your parents from spilling over into the way you parent your own children?*

Psychologist John Bowlby's evolutionary theory of attachment suggests that children come into the world biologically pre-programmed to form attachments with others because this helps them to survive. Whatever the attachment, it becomes a prototype for all future social relationships and allows individuals to predict, control, and manipulate interactions with others.[59]

If you didn't experience a secure attachment with one or more parents, you may carry deep-seated insecurities into adulthood about whether you are deserving of love. This insecurity can have a profound impact on your ability to love and parent your own children. In other words, not having a secure attachment as a child can affect your ability to foster a secure attachment with your offspring.

Perhaps you find it difficult to control your emotions or to know how to self-soothe when you are stressed. Maybe you find it hard to relax or trust others. If you don't have kids yet but are considering it for the future, you might worry about how you will overcome such challenges. Or, it is possible that you've made a conscious decision not to have children specifically because you feel uneasy about your parenting ability.

The good news is: when you become conscious of this dynamic, it becomes easier to move from self-blame and an insecure model of close relationships to a more tolerant, compassionate view of your upbringing.

Once you realize that you didn't deserve the poor treatment of your parents, you will be one step closer to forgiving them. With forgiveness comes a softening of the heart and a real desire to be the best parent you can be for your little ones. To break the cycle of raising your children with an insecure attachment, you will need to change your perspective. This could involve seeing your parents as ill-equipped to create the kind of family environment that fostered confidence and secure attachments. Hopefully, it will become clear that you are not the same as them.

Saying, "They did the best they could" may not seem like a satisfactory explanation if you grew up with parents who caused you a significant amount of pain. However, trying to move toward that perspective can bring you three key benefits:

- You may be able to successfully establish a more satisfying relationship with your parents instead of being estranged from them.

- You will be in a better position to set reasonable limits in your new relationship with them, especially if they continue to exhibit negative behavior.

- When you gain a different perspective on why your parents behaved as they did, it can help you to avoid repeating the cycle of insecure attachments with your own children.

Generational pain is a relentless cycle. The emotional imprints stamped on your psyche from traumatic experiences, unresolved conflicts, or unhealed pain are often invisible. Once you understand that these wounds are influencing your behaviors, beliefs, and relationships, you can step up to correct them and break the pattern.

Analyzing the cycle of pain

Intergenerational wounds perpetuate a cycle of suffering—anger, bitterness, criticism, and holding onto grudges become the currency of this pattern. This can impact family dynamics, relationships, and your well-being.

Breaking free from this cycle necessitates a profound shift in your perspective and embracing the potent remedy of forgiveness. Here is a high-level overview of the process:

1. **Acknowledge the pain**: For forgiveness to occur, acknowledge your pain from its roots. Look at your challenges as an adult and identify the deeply embedded patterns of behavior within your family beliefs. If you can fetch yourself from that learned behavior, you can forge a new way of being that is better aligned with your values.

2. **Acknowledge destructive behavior**: Rather than being hyper-critical of yourself and feeling angry all the time—which often leads to self-sabotage—dig deep into the source of negative thoughts and emotions. Many of them will be inherited beliefs and patterns of learned behavior that can overspill onto your family.

3. **Break the cycle**: Make a conscious decision to embrace forgiveness as a way to break the cycle of pain. This is a life-changing moment when the "before" and "after" will soon become apparent, allowing you to create a healthier, more harmonious family.

Forgiveness transcends mere benevolence toward others; it is a profound act of self-liberation and humility. By embracing forgiveness, you break the cycle of pain and remove the emotional shackles tethering you to past traumas. This transformative journey releases you from the burdens of anger and resentment, fosters emotional healing, and paves the way for your children to inherit a legacy of compassion and empathy.

Being mindful of your actions

Most of us spend a large portion of our days on autopilot. From the moment we wake up and have our first sips of coffee to when our heads hit the pillow at night, our days are a combination of learned thoughts, emotions, and actions. If you stop and reflect, you may notice unintended negative impact stemming from some of your automated behaviors. Mindfulness can be a powerful tool for breaking the cycle of learned emotional responses by increasing awareness of our thoughts, emotions, and bodily sensations in the present moment.

Since the way you feel is reflected in how you behave, incorporating a mindful approach to your life will help you to deal with negative emotions that arise—sometimes out of context.

Take the example of Alex, who struggled with crippling feelings of low self-esteem for most of his life. His father was a former major-league football player, and he pushed Alex into the sport at an early age. However, Alex hated football and, as a result, could never live up to his father's expectations. This set the tone within the family, where Alex was made to feel useless and incapable of being "as good as his dad." That feeling stayed with him into his adult life, making it difficult for him to maintain romantic relationships.

When Alex met his girlfriend, Sylvia, he couldn't shake the nagging belief that he wasn't worthy of her affection. Upon looking into ways to help himself break free from this cycle of self-doubt, Alex discovered mindfulness techniques. Starting with simple mindful breathing and meditation exercises, he gradually developed a deeper understanding of his inner self. He learned to observe his thoughts and emotions without judgment, recognize negative self-talk, and challenge the limiting beliefs that had fueled his low self-esteem for so long.

Through mindfulness, Alex was able to change the way he saw himself and his relationship with Sylvia. Instead of constantly seeking her reassurance or doubting her feelings for him, he learned to value himself and trust in her affection. This shifted the dynamic between them, with Alex becoming much more open and communicative—no longer afraid to express his needs and desires for fear of rejection. Rather than trying to hide his vulnerabilities, he started to embrace his authentic self and stopped trying to live up to imagined expectations.

Mindfulness allows you to press the pause button. Then, you can start to gain control over what you feel, think, and do. It helps in the following ways:

- **Increased awareness:** Mindfulness helps you become more aware of your automatic emotional responses. By paying attention to the present moment without judgment, you can identify which emotional reactions are learned responses, such as anger or anxiety, and actively choose how to respond to them with intention.

- **Emotional regulation**: Mindfulness cultivates the ability to regulate emotions by creating space between stimulus and response. When you are faced with a triggering situation, mindfulness helps you to pause, observe your emotional response, and choose a more skillful way to respond. This could be as simple as taking a few deep breaths or practicing positive self-talk.

- **Breaking habitual patterns**: Mindfulness practice is useful in disrupting habitual patterns of emotional reactivity, as it can bring attention to the underlying thoughts and beliefs that drive your responses. When you observe patterns non-judgmentally, you can gain greater insight into the conditioning you have undergone and make conscious choices to break free from emotional habits.

- **Increased resilience**: Regular mindfulness practice strengthens resilience by nurturing the ability to bounce back from difficult emotions and experiences. When faced with a challenge, mindfulness can help you to navigate emotions, cope with stress, and find a sense of calm amidst the turmoil.

- **Enhanced empathy:** Mindfulness encourages a non-judgmental awareness of your own emotions and the emotions of others. Having empathy can help to break the cycle of learned emotional responses, allowing you to respond to others with understanding and compassion, rather than always defaulting to reacting in the ways you have learned.

- **Improved interpersonal relationships**: Mindfulness practice promotes healthier relationships by fostering better communication and emotional regulation, helping you to deal with conflicts and disagreements more effectively. This enables you to build loving relationships based on understanding and compassion.

If you want to bring more mindfulness into your life, the three-minute breathing space is a common mindfulness-based cognitive behavioral therapy technique used by many therapists. You can practice the exercise anytime using the following steps:

1. Ask yourself, "How am I doing right now?" Focus on identifying the thoughts, feelings, and sensations that come up.

2. Bring your awareness to your breath.

3. Assess your physical sensations and notice how they are affecting the rest of your body.

Through practicing mindfulness, you may discover that many of your reactions are unhelpful learned behaviors. The next time frustration leads to lashing out at your loved ones or anger spirals into destructive behavior—stop. Examine your emotions. Breathe in. Check in with how your body is reacting. See if you can mindfully let go of any negative thoughts or behaviors.

Reflection

- *Which aspects of your behavior do you believe are learned responses from childhood?*

- *Can you identify any behavioral patterns you would like to change?*

- *What steps can you take to embrace growth and achieve balance?*

- *What steps can you take to stop the cycle of pain and let go of harmful habits?*

- *Can you think of instances in your life when mindfulness would have helped you to deal with negative emotions?*

As we dive into the final chapter of this book, the time has come to leave the past behind—once and for all. You will find strategies for maintaining your emotional well-being as your new future beckons.

Chapter 10

Moving Forward

"You can't start a new chapter in your life if you keep re-reading the last one."

—Suzy Kassem

ADOPTING A NEW WAY of being is crucial to moving forward. Forgiveness is the transformative step that allows you to cross the bridge into a new paradigm where you can envision a better future.

To get to this brighter future, you must first focus on the present. By investing in the now, you can lay the foundations for happier days ahead. The present is what will determine your success in reaching your future dreams and goals.

Although this chapter is about moving forward, nurturing your current well-being is the first step toward empowerment and self-growth. Like an athlete preparing to run a marathon, you need to do the training—exercise self-discipline, understand the importance of pace, and push yourself to keep going through the challenging times. Ensure you are prepared for the track that lies ahead of you: the track of life.

But don't let this metaphor scare you—you don't have to get up at 5 AM or run ten miles a day to achieve this mindset. There are other, more subtle ways to cultivate emotional well-being that will set you in good stead for the future. The following section will explore one technique that can help enrich your present and prepare you to face the future with a positive outlook.

Finding your purpose

What is your life's purpose? This may sound like a loaded question, but exploring it can shape how you live now and in the future. The Japanese practice of *ikigai* helps you to do just that. It is both an idea and a way of life, similar to what you might call a "vocation" or "purpose." Ikigai is all about living meaningfully—a simple concept with far-reaching effects. In a nutshell, "Ikigai represents the attention we give to the present and the point at which our mission, vocation, and professional lives meet."[60]

Each of us can find our individual path to joy, curiosity, and passion—although identifying our ikigai takes persistence and patience. Life then becomes a joyful, meaningful experience in which the past loses its hold over us as we embrace the true beauty of living in the present.

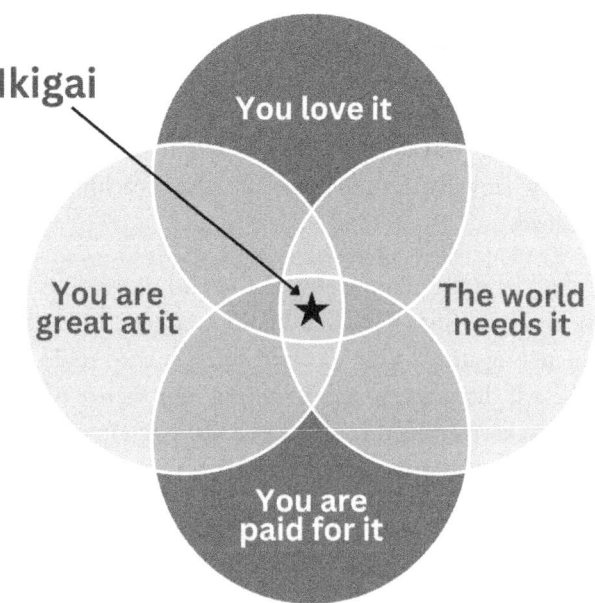

The concept of ikigai contains four fundamental elements:

1. What you love
2. What you are good at
3. What the world needs
4. What you can be paid for

Adhering to the four central elements of ikigai may be a challenge at first. You may be steered off course by the people around you—especially in long-standing relationships with parents or siblings who may not align with your needs, aspirations, and desires.

It's important to remember that you alone can determine your future, and that no one else should dictate how you live your life. Whenever you feel cornered or compromised, refer back to the reasons you connect with your ikigai. The following questions can be used as a guide:

1. What do you love?
   - What brings you joy?
   - What activities capture your interest?
   - When do you feel the happiest?
   - What were you doing the last time you lost track of time?
   - Which experiences leave you feeling invigorated?

2. What are you good at?
   - What skills do you have?
   - What do people ask you for help with?
   - What talents or abilities come naturally to you?

- What do you excel at?

3. What does the world need?
    - What can you offer that would bring value to others?
    - Which societal issues do you feel compelled to address?
    - Will your contributions remain relevant in the future?
    - What areas do you perceive as lacking in society?

4. What can you be paid for?
    - What job could you do to give greater value to the world?
    - What is your dream profession?
    - Which roles, positions, or tasks pique your interest?
    - Do you currently earn a sustainable income?

As you consider each point, look for patterns in your responses and evaluate what is contributing to or hindering your sense of ikigai. This mode of thinking needs time and dedication, but it can eventually lead you to discover your true life purpose while finding joy in the present moment.

Contrary to common belief, ikigai isn't only relevant to your career or how you earn a living. In Japanese culture, it is a way of life that can include hobbies, pastimes, and simple pleasures. Discovering your ikigai involves appreciating the significance and joy found in both small moments and the broader journey of life. Analyzing the past can help you do this to a certain extent; perhaps, try looking back on what you enjoyed doing in your childhood or teenage years. You can then rediscover these passions by reflecting on what gave you pleasure, what interested you, and what gave you a great sense of satisfaction.

The following questions can help point you toward ways you can make subtle shifts to better prioritize your ikigai:

- Are your daily activities primarily centered on the present moment or geared toward future endeavors?

- Do your hobbies, interests, and activities cater solely to your own enjoyment, or do you also share them with others?

- In your daily interactions, do you focus more on giving or receiving? Do you see room for better balancing this dynamic?

- Do you approach life with a flexible mindset that embraces change, or do you find yourself sticking to fixed beliefs and expectations?

- Is your thinking driven solely by logic, or do you also consider and engage with your emotions?

- Do you tend to offer help to strangers or those close to you?

- Are you actively working toward your goals, or passively waiting for them to materialize?

- Can you shift your focus to the world around you, embrace a mindset of openness to change, and allow yourself to fully experience your emotions?

There are no right or wrong answers to these questions, but identifying areas where you can improve will help bring you closer to your ikigai. For example, perhaps you used to enjoy dancing, but you left that passion behind as you got caught up in the world of home, work, and family commitments. In this scenario, it may be worthwhile to explore joining a class at a local dance school or finding out if there are social events focused on dance in your area. Make a point to schedule some element of dance into your weekly rhythm and consider inviting family or friends to join you. Then, see if you are able to discover a long-lost passion that will bring a greater sense of well-being.

Focusing on the present

Ikigai also incorporates the idea of experiencing joy in life's simple moments. Central to this are the practices of mindfulness and curiosity. Even mundane tasks can be done with meaningful intent—engaging you fully and making every present moment significant.

Here is an example of how you can bring mindfulness and curiosity to something as simple as making your daily cup of tea or coffee:

- Focus on making the drink rather than letting your mind wander.

- Pay close attention to smells, sounds, textures, and tastes—such as the smoothness of the cup in your hands and the heat of the beverage.

- Observe your hands as you move through the process, and watch the ways in which the liquid moves.

- Be present in what you are doing and creating.

With these types of exercises, you can cultivate pleasure in even the most mundane tasks.

Sustaining well-being

In previous chapters, we have highlighted the importance of setting boundaries, prioritizing self-care, practicing mindfulness, and focusing on personal growth. These are all vital to maintaining a sense of emotional well-being.

Another way to maintain your well-being is by creating your own personal "blue zone." Blue zones are regions in the world where people statistically have longer-than-average lifespans. Researcher Dan Buettner of National Geographic has extensively studied the "secrets" to longevity and well-being by analyzing the inhabitants of these regions[61], and has narrowed the results down to the following principles:

- Eating a healthy diet
- Regular physical activity
- Strong social connections
- A sense of purpose
- Community involvement

Here are some strategies you can consider implementing to create your personal blue zone:

- **Eating a healthy diet**: Minimize processed foods, sugary drinks, and excessive carbohydrate consumption. Prioritize fresh, locally sourced, and organic foods when possible.

- **Engaging in regular physical activity**: Build exercise into your routine, prioritizing activities you enjoy. This may be walking, cycling, swimming, yoga, dancing, or anything that allows you to move your body.

- **Maintaining strong social connections**: Cultivate meaningful relationships with family and friends. Prioritize spending time with loved ones and giving back to others, even if only in small ways.

- **Gaining a sense of purpose**: Identify activities and pursuits that bring meaning and fulfillment to your life. Get involved in volunteering, engage in creative endeavors, or set meaningful goals.

- **Getting involved with your community**: Prioritize connecting with others through shared interests and activities; nurture supportive social networks.

- **Creating a healthy living environment**: Declutter and organize your space, bring nature inside with plants or natural light, and avoid exposure to environmental toxins.

- **Staying a lifelong learner**: Stay curious and engaged by learning new skills and exploring new interests and hobbies.

Making small tweaks in your lifestyle can promote longevity, health, and happiness in your life. And over time, even minor changes can bring significant improvements in your overall well-being.

Practicing emotional intelligence

Emotional intelligence (sometimes referred to as "EI") is a skill that helps you navigate interpersonal relationships and improve overall well-being. The term was first introduced in the early 1990s by psychologists Peter Salovey and John D. Mayer[62] and later gained mainstream attention through the 1995 book, "Emotional Intelligence: Why It Can Matter More Than IQ" by Daniel Goleman.[63] Goleman expanded on the idea and proposed that emotional intelligence plays a crucial role in personal and professional success—often more so than intellectual ability (IQ).

Emotional intelligence is defined as:

- The ability to **recognize, understand, and manage your emotions**

- The ability to **recognize, understand, and influence the emotions of others**

So, how can you apply emotional intelligence when navigating your future after forgiveness? Many of the ways tie back to concepts explored throughout this book.

- **Begin with self-awareness.**
    - Acknowledging and understanding your past trauma helps

you recognize how your thoughts, emotions, and behaviors are influenced.

- For instance, if you have a pattern of avoidance or emotional detachment when dealing with challenging situations, such behaviors may stem from experiences with your family. Recognizing these patterns will allow you to correct them and foster a more caring and supportive approach to the ways you treat yourself and your loved ones.

- **Learn to regulate your emotions.**

    - Through emotional intelligence, you can learn to manage emotions in healthy ways.

    - This involves identifying triggers and effectively managing overwhelming feelings, such as anxiety or anger.

    - Deep breathing and other mindfulness techniques can help you cope with emotions, particularly if you are feeling overwhelmed in certain situations.

- **Cultivate empathy.**

    - Empathy enables you to understand and connect with the experiences of others, allowing you to offer support and validation to those who need it.

    - Acknowledging and validating your parents' potential childhood trauma can foster healing and understanding.

- **Practice effective communication.**

    - Emotional intelligence involves assertively and empathetically communicating your feelings and needs.

    - This facilitates open dialogue and helps break down barriers to healing.

- ○ When you share personal experiences in a safe environment, you encourage connection and healing with others.

- **Set boundaries.**
  - ○ Establishing healthy boundaries protects you from further harm and preserves your emotional well-being.
  - ○ Emotional intelligence can aid in identifying and asserting boundaries, keeping you safe from family members or anyone else who perpetuates harmful behaviors.

- **Seek support when needed.**
  - ○ Reach out when you are struggling.
  - ○ You can contact a mental health professional, join a support group, or participate in deep conversations with a trusted friend.
  - ○ High emotional intelligence directly correlates with reaching out for help when dealing with complex relationship dynamics.

Emotional intelligence requires self-awareness, empathy, effective communication, and healthy coping strategies. When you develop these traits, you will find yourself better equipped to create a positive future—and set a good example for your children or loved ones.

People with emotional intelligence typically demonstrate a high degree of self-awareness, exhibit self-regulation, show empathy toward others, and possess strong social skills. Additionally, they are more likely to be adaptable, show resilience when faced with challenges, and be adept at problem-solving. If these descriptions don't sound like you, know that these are all skills you can cultivate and learn.

As an example of going from struggling with emotions to forging deep connections through emotional intelligence, consider Emily. Excessive fighting between Emily's parents marked her childhood, so she never learned how to express herself within healthy boundaries. As a result, she felt isolated and lonely growing up, unable to form meaningful relationships due to emotional baggage. She longed for connection but didn't know how to open up or let people get close to her. This was a self-perpetuating cycle, as the more distance she maintained, the lonelier she felt.

When Emily stumbled upon the concept of emotional intelligence and delved deeper into the topic, she realized that her relationship struggles were rooted in her inability to understand and regulate her own emotions, as well as an inability to empathize with others. This "aha moment" helped her to see what she needed to change—she sought help from a therapist and began a journey of growth. Upon gaining greater understanding of why she behaved in the ways she did, she was able to start turning her life around.

Emily honed her communication skills and learned how to express her thoughts and feelings with clarity and empathy. She also embraced vulnerability, allowing herself to be seen and understood by others—even when it felt uncomfortable. As she developed emotional intelligence, she was able to form deeper connections with friends and loved ones. Now, she can experience moments of genuine joy and intimacy she had never thought possible. Although Emily still occasionally feels the urge to close herself off from others, she now makes a conscious effort to correct her behavior and pursue closeness when desired.

Structured self-reflection

The Naikan Method is a practice borrowed from Buddhism, first introduced to the west by psychotherapist David Reynolds.[64] The idea was later developed by the leading authority on Japanese psychology, Gregg Krech, in his book, "Naikan: Gratitude, Grace, and the Japanese Art of Self-Reflection."[65]

The Japanese word *naikan* means "looking inside or seeing oneself with the mind's eye," and the practice encourages individuals to step back and reflect on the life they are living.

Krech describes naikan as being a structured form of self-reflection that encourages and helps us to understand:

- Ourselves

- Our relationships with others

- The fundamental nature of human existence[66]

The Naikan Method is relatively simple, requiring you to reflect on the people in your life and ask three questions:

1. What have you received from them?

2. What have you given them?

3. What troubles or difficulties have you caused them?

Through this examination, you can gain the opportunity to develop a profound sense of gratitude for acts of kindness bestowed upon you by others.

When you ask yourself what you have received from others (you can include both people you know and complete strangers), what comes to mind? To get the most out of this exercise, it is important to slow down long enough to see things you might normally miss. *Who smiled at you today, helped you out, or took an action that benefited you?* It may be the person selling tickets at the train station, the neighbor who greets you with a "good morning" every day, or your colleague who helps you out regularly with tasks.

Thinking about the gifts you receive each day—no matter how small—can fill you with a sense of genuine gratitude.

When you ask yourself what you have given to others, the answers can have a profound effect on how you feel about yourself and life in general. *Did you give up your seat to someone on the bus, hold a door open, or leave an extra tip for a waiter?* Every action has a reaction, and the goodness you radiate will give you satisfaction and a sense of worth.

The last question to ask yourself is what troubles and difficulties you have caused others. It might be difficult to admit that you have caused someone upset or harm—either directly or indirectly—but self-awareness requires you to hold yourself accountable for your actions. Krech explains, "If we are not willing to see and accept those events in which we have been the source of others' suffering, then we cannot truly know ourselves or the grace by which we live."[67]

Taking this practice a step further, try picturing yourself near the end of your life, looking back at the way you lived. *What do you see? Do you see a person who took more than they gave?* It's a sobering thought, and one that can help you to rethink how you live in the present. Instead of waiting until it is too late, you can improve yourself and your relationships with others through self-awareness and reflection now.

By acknowledging past mistakes and expressing gratitude for the kindnesses you have experienced, you can cultivate a sense of purpose, resilience, and inner peace. This heightened self-awareness and gratitude can lead to more fulfilling relationships, improved mental well-being, and a greater capacity to face life's challenges with optimism and resilience.

Reflection

- *What is something you loved to do when you were younger that you would like to try doing again?*
- *What activities fill you with a sense of joy?*
- *When was the last time you focused on the present moment?*
- *What minor changes can you make in your life to improve your physical health and well-being?*
- *How aware are you of your emotions and the emotions of others?*
- *Acknowledge one thing you have received from someone today.*
- *Acknowledge one thing you have given someone today.*

Conclusion

As you wrap up this book, it's my sincere hope that you feel better prepared to face the future with a lighter heart. While the journey to forgiveness isn't easy, it has the potential to lead you toward a brighter and fuller life.

Understanding the impact of our childhood experiences is the first step toward decoding our current behaviors. By recognizing our emotional baggage and determining our attachment styles, we can begin to draw connections between prior events and current thought processes.

Next, we must internalize the importance of forgiveness. With benefits including raised self-esteem and reduced anxiety, forgiveness is a worthwhile pursuit for our own well-being. It's also important to note that forgiveness doesn't equal reconciliation; it's possible to forgive even if rebuilding a relationship is out of the question.

Confronting our painful emotions will involve digging beneath the surface to discover which feelings are hidden underneath. Once we've uncovered these, we can learn to better identify our triggers. And, over time, we can continue to shift our perspectives to remove resentment and take back our power.

Fostering empathy is a delicate balance, as taking on the weight of too many emotions from other people can cause our well-being to suffer. However, challenging ourselves to truly understand different points of view can bring significant benefit. Putting ourselves in someone else's shoes allows us to find common ground and makes it easier to move toward forgiveness.

Setting and holding boundaries is a crucial part of navigating relationships, and it's especially vital in connections with family members. Limits help to ensure that our own needs don't fall to the wayside, so it's important to consider our well-being in all areas of life when determining boundaries. In some cases, this may involve cutting ties to preserve our mental capacity.

Cultivating self-compassion allows us to learn from our experiences while protecting our mental health. Then, we can utilize a similar skillset to extend compassion to our parents, bringing us closer to adopting a forgiving mindset.

Continuing the forgiveness journey, it will be important to examine motivations. Distancing ourselves from blame can allow us to come closer to experiencing altruistic love, which will bring the greatest possibility for successfully forgiving those who've hurt us.

While rebuilding a relationship after forgiving isn't always possible, it can result in enhanced well-being when done authentically. If you decide that reconciliation is a path you'd like to pursue with your parent(s), it will be important to first ensure that you have realistic expectations in place.

Bringing mindfulness to your actions is a helpful way to avoid automatic responses. Although it can take time to fully stop repeating learned behaviors, holding yourself accountable with increased awareness can help you break the cycle of generational trauma.

Finally, as you move forward, finding purpose can help you live the most meaningful life. Further, focusing on sustaining your physical and emotional well-being will complement your positive mindset gained through forgiveness.

As you embark on the next chapter of your life, remember that the power to heal lies within you. Forgiveness is not only an act of mercy, but an invaluable gift to yourself.

The movie "Philomena" portrays an example of the power of forgiveness. The story follows a woman's quest to find her missing son after he was given up for adoption by Catholic nuns without her consent. Philomena returns to the convent 50 years later to confront the nuns, accompanied by reporter Sixsmith who is outraged at the injustice of the atrocious acts. Sixsmith bursts into the convent and begins to unleash on one of the nuns, but Philomena intervenes. What happens next is unexpected.

Philomena tells the nun that she has forgiven her.

Sixsmith, in exasperation, turns to Philomena and says, "Just like that?" to which she answers, "No, not just like that."

She ends by telling him, "...I don't want to hate people. I don't want to be like you. Look at you."

"I'm angry," Sixsmith responds vehemently.

"Must be exhausting!" Philomena replies.

As you reflect on the insights gained throughout these chapters, consider which strategies are most relevant to your situation. Embrace the power of empathy, compassion, and understanding. Set aside resentment and bitterness, and open your heart to the possibility of renewal.

Forgiveness is a journey that requires courage, vulnerability, and resilience. The final destination holds the promise of liberation, healing, and profound personal growth.

Dare to forgive, and in doing so, you'll discover the transformative power of grace, compassion, and unconditional love.

Thank You

I'm honored you've made it all the way to the end of my book. I sincerely hope you've come away with the knowledge and skills you need to free yourself from resentment—for your parents or anyone else who's done you wrong.

The best way to support an independent author like me is by leaving an honest review. If you can spare a minute, please use these QR codes below to share what you thought about my book while it's still fresh in your mind. Thank you!

Leave a review on Amazon US:

Leave a review on Amazon UK:

ABOUT THE AUTHOR

Selma Geis studied psychology and philosophy before embarking on a 20-year teaching career while raising her two now-grown sons. She draws on her lifelong experience in the educational sector and her own personal journey toward forgiveness to help all those wanting to free themselves from unhealthy parental ties. Her goal is to provide practical strategies for anyone wishing to move toward a place of forgiveness and fulfillment, whatever their parental upbringing.

Selma was inspired to write about the importance of forgiveness after her own experience of growing up with an abusive father. Unable to forgive or forget, it wasn't until his death that she began to work through her feelings of anger and resentment that had accumulated over the years. Through researching current insights into the psychology of parental forgiveness and attending seminars by leading voices on the subject, Selma eventually came to terms with her father's "unforgivable" behavior. She was able to release herself of the negative emotions that such unhealthy relationships create and move toward a place of healing, compassion, and empowerment.

When Selma is not helping both parents and youngsters to improve their relationships through her advisory work in the educational sphere, she frequently writes articles and blogs for various parenting websites. Touching on topics such as setting boundaries, moving from victimhood to empowerment, and strategies for dealing with childhood trauma, Selma hopes to inspire her readership to take control of their own lives by replacing bitterness with forgiveness.

Selma lives just outside of Boston, where she enjoys getting creative in the kitchen and taking long walks with her four-legged friend, Max.

REFERENCES

1. Mikulincer, M., & Shaver, P. (2013). Attachment Theory as a Framework for a Positive Psychology of Love. *M. Hojjat, and Duncan Cramer (eds), Positive Psychology of Love.* https://doi.org/10.1093/acprof:oso/9780199791064.003.0006

2. Worthington, E.L., & Sandage, S.J. (2015). *Forgiveness and Spirituality in Psychotherapy: A Relational Approach.*

3. Enright, R.D., & Fitzgibbons, R. (2015). *Forgiveness Therapy.*

4. Johns Hopkins University. (n.d.). *Forgiveness: Your Health Depends on It.* https://www.hopkinsmedicine.org/health/wellness-and-prevention/forgiveness-your-health-depends-on-it

5. McCullough, M. E., Worthington, E. L., Jr., & Rachal, K. C. (1997). Interpersonal forgiving in close relationships. *Journal of Personality and Social Psychology, 73(2), 321–336.* https://doi.org/10.1037/0022-3514.73.2.321

6. Stackhouse, M., Ross, R., & Boon, S. (2016). The devil in the details: Individual differences in unforgiveness and health correlates. *Personality and Individual Differences,* Volume 94, 2016, Pages 337-341, ISSN 0191-8869. https://doi.org/10.1016/j.paid.2016.02.005

7. National Institute for the Clinical Application of Behavioral Medicine. (n.d.). *How Anger Affects Your Brain and Body.* https://www.nicabm.com/brain-how-anger-affects-your-brain-and-body-part-1

8. BetterHealth. (n.d.). *Anger - how it affects people.* https://www.betterhealth.vic.gov.au/health/healthyliving/anger-how-it-affects-people#physical-effects-of-anger

9. Rachman, S. (2009). *Betrayal: a psychological analysis.* Behav Res Ther. 2010 Apr;48(4):304-11. doi: 10.1016/j.brat.2009.12.002. Epub 2009 Dec 24. PMID: 20035927.

10. Tzieropoulos, H., de Peralta, R., Bossaerts, P., & Gonzalez Andino, S. L. (2011). The impact of disappointment in decision making: inter-individual differences and electrical neuroimaging. *Frontiers In Human Neuroscience,* doi: 10.3389/fnhum.2010.00235.

11. Alvis, L., Zhang, N., Sandler, I.N., & Kaplow, J.B. (2022). Developmental Manifestations of Grief in Children and Adolescents: Caregivers as Key Grief Facilitators. *J Child Adolesc Trauma.* 2022 Jan 28;16(2):447-457. doi: 10.1007/s40653-021-00435-0. PMID: 35106114; PMCID: PMC8794619.

12. Mukherjee, K. (2022). *Childhood trauma and its effects in adulthood.* 10.13140/RG.2.2.10356.42889.

13. Silvia, P., & Phillips, A. (2011). Evaluating self-reflection and insight as self-conscious traits. *Personality and Individual Differences,* Volume 50, Issue 2, 2011, Pages 234-237, ISSN 0191-8869, https://doi.org/10.1016/j.paid.2010.09.035

14. Almeida, B., & Cunha, C. (2023). Time, Resentment, and Forgiveness: Impact on the Well-Being of Older Adults. *Trends in Psychol.* https://doi.org/10.1007/s43076-023-00 343-2

15. Forster, D. E., Billingsley, J., Russell, V. M., McCauley, T. G., Smith, A., Burnette, J. L., Ohtsubo, Y., Schug, J., Lieberman, D., & McCullough, M. E. (2020). Forgiveness takes place on an attitudinal continuum from hostility to friendliness: Toward a closer union of forgiveness theory and measurement. *Journal of Personality and Social Psychology,* 119(4), 861–880. https://doi.org/10.1037/pspi0000227

16. Witvliet, C. V. O., Ludwig, T. E., & Laan, K. L. V. (2001). Granting forgiveness or harboring grudges: Implications for emotion, physiology, and health. *Psychological Science,* 12(2), 117-123.

17. Zaki, J. (2019). *The War for Kindness: Building Empathy in a Fractured World.* Crown.

18. Buffone, A., & Poulin, M. (2014). Empathy, Target Distress, and Neurohormone Genes Interact to Predict Aggression for Others-Even Without Provocation. *Personality & social psychology bulletin.* 40. 1406-22. DOI: 10.1177/0146167214549320.

19. Hodges, S. D., Kiel, K. J., Kramer, A. D. I., Veach, D., & Villanueva, B. R. (2010). Giving Birth to Empathy: The Effects of Similar Experience on Empathic Accuracy, Empathic Concern, and Perceived Empathy. *Personality and Social Psychology Bulletin,* 36(3), 398-409. https://doi.org/10.1177/0146167209350326

20. Mar, R. A. (2018). Stories and the Promotion of Social Cognition. *Current Directions in Psychological Science,* 27(4), 257-262. https://doi.org/10.1177/0963721417749654

21. Seppälä, E. M., Simon-Thomas, E., Brown, S., Worline, M, Cameron, C, & Doty, J. (2017). *The Oxford Handbook of Compassion Science, Oxford Library of Psychology.* https://doi.org/10.1093/oxfordhb/9780190464684.001.0001

22. Lichtenfeld, S., Buechner, V.L., Maier, M.A., & Fernández-Capo, M. (2015). Forgive and Forget: Differences between Decisional and Emotional Forgiveness. *PLoS One.*10(5):e01 25561. doi: 10.1371/journal.pone.0125561. PMID: 25946090; PMCID: PMC4422736.

23. Grassini, S. (2022). A Systematic Review and Meta-Analysis of Nature Walk as an Intervention for Anxiety and Depression. *J Clin Med.* 11(6):1731. doi: 10.3390/jcm11061731. PMID: 35330055; PMCID: PMC8953618.

24. British Association for Counselling and Psychotherapy. (2020). *What do counsellors and psychotherapists mean by boundaries?.* https://www.bacp.co.uk/media/8273/bacp-bound aries-client-information-sheet-april-2020.pdf

25. Katherine, A. (2010). *Boundaries: Where you end and I begin.* Hazelden Publishing.

26. Blatt, S. J. (2008). *Polarities of experience: Relatedness and self-definition in personality development, psychopathology, and the therapeutic process.* American Psychological Association.

27. Davies, P. T., Cummings, E. M., & Winter, M. A. (2004). Pathways between profiles of family functioning, child security in the interparental subsystem, and child psychological problems. *Development and Psychopathology*, 16, 525–550.

28. Carreau, G. (2023). *Understanding Self-Abandonment & How to Overcome It For Good.* WikiHow. https://www.wikihow.com/Self-Abandonment

29. American Psychological Association. (2019). *Mindfulness meditation: A research-proven way to reduce stress.* https://www.apa.org/topics/mindfulness/meditation

30. Summer, J. (2024). *8 Health Benefits of Sleep.* Sleep Foundation. https://www.sleepfoundation.org/how-sleep-works/benefits-of-sleep

31. Christ, A. (2021). The influence of excessive use of social media. *Indonesian Journal of Social Sciences* 13(1):11. DOI:10.20473/ijss.v13i1.26351.

32. Agllias, K. (2018). Missing family: The adult child's experience of parental estrangement. *Journal of Social Work Practice*, 32(1), 59–72. https://doi.org/10.1080/02650533.2017.1326471

33. Conti, R.P. (3025). Family estrangement: Establishing a prevalence rate. JPBS. 2015;3(2). doi:10.15640/jpbs.v3n2a4

34. Blake, L. (n.d.). *Hidden voices: Family estrangement in adulthood.* Stand Alone UK, University of Cambridge.

35. Tawwab, N. G. (2021). *Set Boundaries, Find Peace: A Guide to Reclaiming Yourself.* TarcherPerigee.

36. Saarinen, A.I.L., Keltikangas-Järvinen, L., Hintsa, T., Pulkki-Råback, L., Ravaja, N., Lehtimäki, T., Raitakari, O., & Hintsanen, M. (2020). Does Compassion Predict Blood Pressure and Hypertension? The Modifying Role of Familial Risk for Hypertension. *Int J Behav Med.* 27(5):527-538. doi: 10.1007/s12529-020-09866-5. PMID: 32347444; PMCID: PMC7497423.

37. Kucerova, B., Levit-Binnun, N., Gordon, I., & Golland, Y. (2023). *From Oxytocin to Compassion: The Saliency of Distress.* https://doi.org/10.3390/biology12020183

38. Chierchia, G., Singer, T. (2017). *The Neuroscience of Compassion and Empathy and Their Link to Prosocial Motivation and Behavior.* Academic Press. https://doi.org/10.1016/B978-0-12-805308-9.00020-8

39. Neff, K. (2015). *Self-Compassion: The Proven Power of Being Kind to Yourself.* William Morrow Paperbacks.

40. Marshall, S. L., Ciarrochi. J., Parker, P. D., & Sahdra, B. K. (2019). Is Self-Compassion Selfish? The Development of Self-Compassion, Empathy, and Prosocial Behavior in Adolescence. *Journal of Research on Adolescence.* https://doi.org/10.1111/jora.12492

41. Whelton, W. J., & Greenberg, L. S. (2005). Emotion in self-criticism. *Personality and Individual Differences*, 38(7), 1583-1595. https://doi.org/10.1016/j.paid.2004.09.024

42. Ekman, R., Fletcher, A., Giota, J., Eriksson, A., Thomas, B., & Bååthe, F. (2022). A Flourishing Brain in the 21st Century: A Scoping Review of the Impact of Developing Good Habits for Mind, Brain, Well-Being, and Learning. *Mind, Brain, and Education*, 16: 13-23. https://doi.org/10.1111/mbe.12305

43. Kim, J. J., Payne, E.S., & Tracy, E.L. (2022). Indirect Effects of Forgiveness on Psychological Health Through Anger and Hope: A Parallel Mediation Analysis. *J Relig Health.* 61(5):3729-3746. doi: 10.1007/s10943-022-01518-4. Epub 2022 Feb 21. PMID: 35190955; PMCID: PMC10120569.

44. Worthington, E. L. (2003). *Five Steps to Forgiveness: The Art and Science of Forgiving.* Crown Publishers.

45. Li, H., Wade, N.G., & Worthington, E. L. (2020). Editorial: Understanding the Processes Associated With Forgiveness. *Front Psychol.* 11:628185. doi: 10.3389/fpsyg.2020.628185. PMID: 33408678; PMCID: PMC7779586.

46. Davis, D. E., Yang, X., DeBlaere, C., McElroy, S. E., Van Tongeren, D. R., Hook, J. N., & Worthington, E. L. (2016). The injustice gap. *Psychology of Religion and Spirituality*, 8(3), 175–184. https://doi.org/10.1037/rel0000042

47. Lichtenfeld, S., Maier, M. A., Buechner, V. L., & Fernández Capo, M. (2019). The Influence of Decisional and Emotional Forgiveness on Attributions. *Frontiers in Psychology, VOL.10.* https://doi.org/10.3389/fpsyg.2019.01425

48. Thomas, P.A., Liu, H., & Umberson, D. (2017). Family Relationships and Well-Being. *Innov Aging.* 2017 Nov;1(3):igx025. doi: 10.1093/geroni/igx025. Epub 2017 Nov 11. PMID: 29795792; PMCID: PMC5954612.

49. Salihovic, A., Mahmutovic, J., Brankovic, S., Pindžo, E., Hajrovic, A., & Mrkulić, E. (2021). The Connection Between The Family Environment And The Mental Health Of An Individual. *European Journal of Biomedical and Pharmaceutical Sciences.*

50. Grevenstein, D., Bluemke, M., Schweitzer, J., & Aguilar-Raab, C. (2019). Better family relationships--higher well-being: The connection between relationship quality and health related resources. *Mental Health & Prevention,* Volume 14, 2019, 200160, ISSN 2212-6570, https://doi.org/10.1016/j.mph.2019.200160

51. Kennison, S., & Spooner, V. (2020). Childhood relationships with parents and attachment as predictors of resilience in young adults. *Journal of Family Studies.* 29. 1-13. 10.1080/13229400.2020.1861968.

52. Tobin, E., Slatcher, R., & Robles, T. (2012). *Family Relationships and Physical Health.* American Psychological Association.

53. Harvard College. (2019). *An active social life may help you live longer.* https://www.hsph.harvard.edu/news/hsph-in-the-news/active-social-life-longevity

54. Chen, P., & Harris, K. M. (2019). Association of Positive Family Relationships With Mental Health Trajectories From Adolescence to Midlife. *JAMA Pediatr.* 2019 Dec 1;173(12):e193336. doi: 10.1001/jamapediatrics.2019.3336. Epub 2019 Dec 2. PMID: 31589247; PMCID: PMC6784807.

55. Grevenstein, D., Bluemke, M., Schweitzer, J., & Aguilar-Raab, C. (2019). Better family relationships--higher well-being: The connection between relationship quality and health related resources. *Mental Health & Prevention,* Volume 14, 2019, 200160, ISSN 2212-6570, https://doi.org/10.1016/j.mph.2019.200160

56. Harvey, J. H., & Omarzu, J. (1997). Minding the close relationship. *Personality and social psychology review: an official journal of the Society for Personality and Social Psychology, Inc,* 1(3), 224–240. https://journals.sagepub.com/doi/10.1207/s15327957pspr0103_3

57. Mcleod, S. (2024). *Albert Bandura's Social Learning Theory.* Simply Psychology. https://www.simplypsychology.org/bandura.html

58. LaMorte, W. W. (2019). *Behavioral change models.* Boston University School of Public Health. https://sphweb.bumc.bu.edu/otlt/mph-modules/sb/behavioralchangetheories/behavioralchangetheories5.html

59. Holmes, J. (2014). *John Bowlby and Attachment Theory (Makers of Modern Psychotherapy).* Routledge.

60. Mitsuhashi, Y. (2018). *Ikigai: The Japanese Art of a Meaningful Life.* Kyle Books.

61. Buettner, D. (n.d.). *Blue Zones.* https://danbuettner.com/blue-zones

62. Salovey, P., & Mayer, J. D. (1990). Emotional Intelligence. *Imagination, Cognition and Personality,* 9(3), 185-211. https://doi.org/10.2190/DUGG-P24E-52WK-6CDG

63. Goleman, D. (1997). *Emotional Intelligence: Why It Can Matter More Than IQ.* Bantam.

64. Reynolds, D. (1983). *Naikan Psychotherapy: Meditation for Self-Development.* University of Chicago Press.

65. Krech, G. (2001). *Naikan: Gratitude, Grace, and the Japanese Art of Self-Reflection.* Stone Bridge Press.

66. Sutton, J. (2021). *Naikan Therapy: Applying the Japanese Art of Self-Reflection.* PositivePsychology. https://positivepsychology.com/naikan-therapy

67. Krech, G. (2017). *Question Your Life: Naikan Self-Reflection and the Transformation of Our Stories.* ToDo Institute.

Printed in Great Britain
by Amazon